The World Economy in Transition

Also by Michael Beenstock

The Foreign Exchanges: Theory, Modelling and Policy (1978)
A Neoclassical Analysis of Macroeconomic Policy (1980)
Health, Migration and Development (1980)

The World Economy in Transition

Michael Beenstock

City University Business School, London

London
GEORGE ALLEN & UNWIN
Boston   Sydney

George Allen & Unwin (Publishers) Ltd,
40 Museum Street, London WC1A, 1LU, UK

George Allen & Unwin (Publishers) Ltd
Park Line, Hemel Hempstead, Herts HP2 4TE, UK

Allen & Unwin Inc.,
9 Winchester Terrace, Winchester, Mass 01890, USA

George Allen & Unwin Australia Pty Ltd,
8 Napier Street, North Sydney, NSW 2060, Australia

First published in 1983

British Library Cataloguing in Publication Data

Beenstock, Michael
  The world economy in transition.
1. Economic history
I. Title
330.9   HC21

ISBN 0-04-339033-1

Library of Congress Cataloging in Publication Data

Beenstock, Michael, 1946-
  The world economy in transition.

Bibliography: p.
Includes index.
1. Economic history—1971-   I. Title.
HC59.B42 1983   330.9′048   82-16469
ISBN 0-04-339033-1

Set in 11 on 12pt Times by Pretace Limited, Salisbury, Wilts.
and printed in Great Britain by Biddles Ltd, Guildford, Surrey

Preface

It is with some hesitation that I admit that the central thesis in this book is rather grand and embraces numerous disciplines ranging from economic history to modern econometrics. The problem with grand theses is that they require decades to investigate and their inter-disciplinary nature means that they run the risk of trespassing upon the specialised territories of others. Since I do not have the necessary decades to devote to the subject of growth and change in the world economy I took the view that it was better to set down the basic ideas on paper rather than to leave them to gather dust upon the shelves. This inevitably means that there are numerous loose ends. More charitably it means that there are fertile research seams to be mined in the future. Therefore the book is no more than a *prima facie* investigation and it is partly for this reason that I detach myself, from time to time, from some of the arguments that I develop in the book.

The central theme of the relationship between the rich and poor countries reflects my professional experience having worked on both sides of the great divide that separates North from South. It also reflects my experiences in the practical world and in academia, especially the former. However, its focus is to explain economic developments in the North rather than the South but I felt that this was impossible without explicitly recognising the changing role of the developing countries in the world economy.

I am grateful for having had the opportunity of presenting seminars at various institutions but especially at the LINK conference in Perugia in 1980 under Larry Klein's chairmanship. I would also like to thank Jim Ball, Sam Brittan,

Forest Capie, Ed Denison, Simon Kuznets and Arthur Lewis for their comments. Chapter 7 is jointly written with Geoffrey Dicks and I am greatly obliged to him for this. I would also like to thank Patrick Willcocks whose research assistance was especially helpful in the early stages and Peter Warburton who helped me in the final stage. Finally I wish to thank Margo Berry who typed the bulk of the manuscript.

Michael Beenstock
London, April 1982

Contents

List of Tables

List of Figures

1

Sea Change in the West

I Developed Countries

The High Tide of Prosperity

The 1970s was a turbulent decade for the world economy in
general and for OECD countries in particular, with more
inflation and less economic growth than in the 1950s and
1960s. Although commentators are always quick to speak of
economic crises there was fairly broad agreement in the late
1960s that the world economy was set for sustained and
stable economic growth over the decades ahead. The cause
for this optimism lay in numerous related factors. First and
foremost, perhaps, was the experience of two decades of
unprecedented economic growth (see Table 1.3) which to
varying degrees had been shared by all the industrialised
countries. At the same time unemployment had remained
persistently low, apart from minor cyclical fluctuations.
World trade – which had been destroyed by interwar protectionism and the economic disruption of the Second World
War – had recovered and was growing at a historically high
rate.

This economic performance bore no resemblance to the
world economy in the two decades following the Second
World War, where in contrast sluggish economic growth,
declining international trade and high unemployment were
experienced by most industrialised countries. Nor was it
regarded as fortuitous, for there was a broad body of optimism (which still persists) that the 1950s and 1960s were a
product of Keynesian economic engineering. Indeed, there
was no reason why the prosperity of the international

economy should not continue as long as appropriate Keynesian policies were pursued both domestically and internationally.

There were few, if any, in the late 1960s who foresaw that international economic prosperity was under threat. It is true that there were some prophets of doom (this is always so in economics), but they had rather different worries. First, there were the international monetary reformers, such as Triffin, who correctly foresaw that the gold exchange system which established the US dollar as the principal reserve currency was inherently unstable. US balance of payments deficits, which were required to meet the demand for international liquidity under fixed exchange rates, were also bound in time to undermine international confidence in the dollar. A time would come when the dollar would no longer command the confidence invested in gold. That time was formally reached in August 1971 when President Nixon relinquished the tie between gold and the dollar. With it the Bretton Woods system was swept away, never to return, despite some vainglorious attempts by the IMF which had the greatest vested interest in fixed exchange rates.

Secondly, there were those who argued that the Vietnam War, or rather the way the US government was financing it, would fuel worldwide inflation which would put an end to the years of prosperity. According to this view, deficit financing would tend to raise the rate of monetary growth in the US which under the fixed exchange rates of Bretton Woods would generate higher rates of monetary growth internationally, thus generating worldwide inflation.

To some extent these two views were related and both were vindicated by subsequent events. As already noted, the dollar ceased to be a substitute for gold and, as will be discussed (see p. 184) US monetary growth undoubtedly contributed to world inflation, although it was not the only cause. But neither of these would be likely to put an end to world economic prosperity. On the contrary, it is arguable that floating exchange rates would be more conducive to economic growth since they introduce a greater element of price flexibility in the workings of the international economy. Nor does economic theory suggest that inflation necessarily undermines economic growth, especially when it has been fully anticipated.

The 1970s

At first the international recession in the early 1970s was regarded as a cyclical phenomenon that required expansionary Keynesian remedies. Table 1.1 indicates that in 1970 unemployment in industrialised countries began to rise while output growth began to decline in 1969. At the same time world trade growth began to falter. These indicators had all the hallmarks of a cyclical recession and Table 1.1 shows that governments somewhat belatedly pursued expansionary fiscal and monetary policies, especially in 1971. As Table 1.2 indicates, the recovery from this recession was short-lived and by previous standards the 1970s were in continuous recession. Nor has the start of the 1980s indicated any break with the trend established in the 1970s.

During the course of the 1970s it was gradually realised that something had changed and that the economic factors

Table 1.1   *The recession of 1970–1*

	1966	1967	1968	1969	1970	1971	1972	1973
Unemployment (%)	2.5	2.8	2.9	2.7	3.1	3.6	3.7	3.3
Annual percentage growth								
GDP	5.4	3.8	5.7	5.2	3.6	3.7	5.5	6.2
Industrial production	6.5	3.7	7.1	7.7	2.0	1.0	6.9	9.3
Government expenditure	6.9	6.5	3.3	1.7	1.9	1.7	3.2	3.0
World trade	7.3	4.9	11.6	12.0	8.6	7.9	8.5	12.3
Money supply	6.2	5.5	7.9	7.0	6.0	11.3	11.9	10.6
Inflation (% p.a.)	3.5	2.9	3.9	4.8	5.6	5.2	4.7	7.7
Proportionate fiscal deficit (% of GDP)	1.4	1.6	1.7	0.0	1.1	2.2	1.8	1.5

Source: UN, OECD and IMF published data

Table 1.2   *Postwar economic indicators – industrialised countries 1950–80*

	1950–60	1960–70	1970–5	1975–80
Growth rates (% p.a.)				
GDP	4.0	4.9	3.1	4.1
Industrial production	4.7	5.8	2.2	4.1
World trade	5.6	6.9	5.6	5.5
Inflation	1.7	2.9	7.8	8.9
Unemployment (%)	3.4	3.0	3.6	5.3

Source: UN, OECD and IMF published data

that underpinned the prosperity of the 1950s and 1960s had disappeared. Precisely what these factors were, or what had changed, remains highly debatable and will no doubt be a source of wonder for economic historians in the years to come. The picture has been considerably clouded by the OPEC price hikes of 1973–4 and 1978–9 which greatly affected the world economy. Indeed, there are many who believe that but for these price hikes international economic prosperity would have continued and that OPEC must be blamed for the economic malaise in the West.

Others seek socio-political explanations and maintain that the plight of the world economy may be attributed to trade union militancy which spontaneously manifested itself in countries as disparate as Austria and Australia and which was, perhaps, kindled by the 'May Events' in France in 1968. The trouble with this view is that it hardly amounts to a proper theory since the transmission mechanism of militancy is not specified. Others believe that slower growth is to be blamed on big government and excessive government spending. Yet others doggedly argue that Keynesian remedies should still be applied and that government spending is not large enough despite the fact that the 'recession' has now lasted more than a decade. Another *ad hoc* 'hypothesis' is that the microchip is responsible.

In many instances the recession is seen in parochial terms. In this country there is much talk of the 'British Disease'. The Dutch have their own disease. However, individual national economic developments have had much in common and in this book I argue that a global perspective is necessary to understand national developments. This does not rule out the importance of national economic considerations and there may be a residual role for the 'disease' theory after all. However, since the late 1960s the industrialised countries as a whole have experienced growing unemployment, de-industrialisation, higher inflation, lower profits, and so on. Either this is a coincidence and the individual national diseases have produced similar symptoms or the industrialised countries as a whole have been subject to common economic forces. This latter perspective underpins the thesis of this book.

The global perspective proposed below is essentially neoclassical, since it draws on basic neoclassical concepts such as market theory. In particular the roles of commodities, energy, technology and economic relationships with less developed countries (LDCs) in the economic development of the developed countries (DCs) are explored in terms of the application of neoclassical analysis. In this perspective the role of OPEC price hikes is identified, but I argue that the seeds of slower economic growth in the DCs were planted much earlier and that the secular turning point is not in fact 1973, as is often supposed, but sometime during the second half of the 1960s. This means that even in the absence of the oil price hikes the DCs would have moved into a different economic phase during the 1970s; indeed, this phase had already begun by that time.

A Historical Perspective

An important conclusion of this study is that economic growth in the West may not necessarily be permanently impaired by the global developments that are identified. Instead DC growth may be temporarily (i.e. in terms of decades) reduced, while economic restructuring takes place during what may be a protracted period of economic transition. This transition may last a generation or more. In certain cases the level of output may be permanently reduced by some of the developments considered, but not the rate of growth of output.

Despite this fairly optimistic conclusion it is as well to see

Table 1.3   *The growth of world industrial production 1705–1980 (annual average growth rates %)*

1705–85	1.5[a]		
1785–1850	2.6		
. . . .			
1820–40	2.9		
1840–60	3.5		
1860–70	2.9		
1870–1900	3.7		
1900–13	4.2		
1913–29	2.7	1950–60	4.75[b]
1929–38	2.0	1960–70	5.75
1938–48	4.1	1970–80	3.2
1948–71	5.6		

Sources: (a) Rostow (1978) p. 49
(b) UN data for Developed Market Economies

the economic growth of the 1950s and 1960s in historical perspective. Table 1.3 shows that the sustained rate of growth of world industrial production in the postwar period up to 1971 was unprecedented, surpassing even the growth rates that were achieved during the first and second industrial revolutions. Table 1.3 further shows that the 1960s proved to be a particularly expansionist decade while in contrast the 1970s saw a sharp decline in growth. Nevertheless this latter was still higher than the long-run average growth rate. The table therefore reminds us that the postwar growth rates may be the exception rather than the rule and that the performance of the 1960s cannot serve as a representative benchmark for judging growth performance. On the other hand, Table 1.3 does not necessarily imply that even higher growth rates cannot be attained in the future.

II   Developing Countries

Reverse Causality

As will be explained later in this chapter (see p. 14), economic developments in the LDCs have had a major influence upon developments in the industrialised countries.

This may sound like the tail wagging the dog; it certainly reverses traditional views about the causal relationship between the DCs and LDCs. The traditional view has been that the industrialised countries are the engine of growth for the LDCs; economic expansion in OECD countries triggers economic growth in LDCs. This view is traditional in the sense that it is reflected in policy statements by politicians and development experts. In addition it is reflected in the structure of various econometric models of the world economy, e.g. Hicks (1976), Beenstock and Minford (1976) and Professor Klein's LINK model.

The traditional view of the causal economic relationships between the developed and the developing countries may roughly be summarised as follows:

(1)   Economic growth in LDCs is assumed to be constrained by the balance of payments. Hence further LDC growth would generate insurmountable balance of payments problems for LDCs.
(2)   Economic growth in developed countries improves the balance of payments for two reasons. First, the demand for LDC exports rises. Second, economic growth tends to raise commodity prices so that the LDC's barter terms of trade improve. Beenstock and Dicks (1981) estimate that when OECD industrial output rises by 1 per cent, relative (to manufactures) commodity prices rise by more than 3 per cent on world markets.
(3)   The improved balance of payments reduces the constraints on LDC growth.
(4)   The higher LDC growth increases LDC imports from OECD countries. This stimulates OECD economic activity and it is plain to see that the LDC 'loop' in the model generates a multiplier effect with regard to the level of world economic activity.

This last stage implies feedback from LDCs to OECD countries, but this is not autonomous. Nevertheless the Brandt Report (1980) has emphasised that in principle the LDCs could serve as an expansionary element in the world economy on the basis of stage 4.

A fundamental criticism of the traditional view is that

stage 1 cannot be taken for granted and the so-called Two Gap Theory of economic development upon which stage 1 is premised is invalid. According to this theory growth is constrained either because savings are inadequate to finance investment (the savings gap), or because exports are not large enough to pay for the imports that growth induces (the foreign exchange gap). In contrast the neoclassical theory of economic development would suggest that neither of these gaps are permanent especially in the medium-term and that they can be closed by interest rate adjustments in the former case and exchange rate adjustments in the latter. For example, the foreign exchange gap can be narrowed by improved competitiveness in trade in manufactures. Therefore the theoretical premises of the two gap theory are open to question and the empirical premises may be in doubt too. The two gap theory is essentially a 'Keynesian' theory of the development process although, as in many other instances, Keynes himself never expressed a view on the matter.

In rejecting the Keynesian approach in favour of the neoclassical approach we admit to the possibility that economic developments in the LDC bloc may affect the OECD economies. The enormous economic transformations in the LDCs over the last two decades in particular seem likely to have altered the balance of world market forces. Rapid LDC industrialisation and rural–urban migration have not had a neutral effect on the world economy. An important thesis in this book is that these developments have indeed been reflected in world prices and these prices have in turn changed economic incentives in the OECD bloc. Hence causality is reversed; in contrast to the traditional view, LDC shocks affect economic developments in the OECD bloc. More generally (and sensibly) the causality is two-way.

Growth in Developing Countries 1950–80

The picture painted in Section I for the OECD was rather grim as from the late 1960s, but the opposite applied to LDCs. The world recession seems to have passed them by. Their growth has continued unabated since the late 1960s and may even have accelerated. All the forecasters have been confounded since, according to the traditional view,

Table 1.4 *Growth performance of developing market economies 1950–80 (average growth % p.a.)*

	GDP	Industrial production	Manufacturing output
1950–55	4.7	6.5	7.0
1955–60	4.3	8.9	7.4
1960–65	5.5	8.2	7.1
1965–70	6.1	9.7	8.2
1970–75	6.2	5.1	7.0
1975–80	5.7[a]	3.9	4.8
AVERAGE	5.4 (4.2)	7.0 (4.5)	6.9

Source: *Statistical Yearbook* (New York: UN) various issues
Note: [a]1975–8

the OECD recession which started in the late 1960s should have transmitted itself to the LDC bloc. In addition the OPEC oil price explosion should in theory have further constrained LDC balance of payments, which would have reduced economic growth yet again. Instead the LDCs as a whole have forged ahead. As will be noted in Chapter 3, this success story is not uniform. However, the exceptions are not sufficiently important to invalidate the basic thesis.

Table 1.4 summarises LDC growth performance over the last three decades. All growth rates have remained high. For purposes of comparison the growth rates for the Developed Market Economies (OECD bloc) are shown in parenthesis. Note that from the mid 1960s output growth in the LDC bloc rises and continues to remain high well beyond the commencement of the OECD recession. During the 1970s GDP growth is half a point above its postwar average, while in the OECD bloc GDP growth was half a point below its postwar average through the 1970s. Note also that during the second half of the 1960s industrial and manufacturing output growth accelerated from its already high level and in manufacturing this growth was sustained into the 1970s. Between 1963 and 1973 manufacturing output grew at an annual average rate of no less than 8·6 per cent. However, during the second half of the 1970s these astonishingly rapid growth rates were not sustained. Table 1.5 shows the differential growth performance of the LDCs *vis à vis* the OECD

Table 1.5 *Differential growth performance 1950–80 (LDC – OECD, % p.a.)*

	GDP	Industrial production	Manufacturing output
1950–60	0.55	2.95	
1960–70	0.85	3.2	1.55
1970–80	2.5	1.2	2.9
AVERAGE	1.3	2.45	

Source: Statistical Yearbook (New York: UN), various issues

bloc. Over the period as a whole LDC growth averaged 28 per cent higher than OECD GDP growth, 54 per cent higher than OECD industrial production growth and 46 per cent higher than the rate of growth of manufacturing output in the OECD. Moreover in the case of GDP and manufacturing the LDCs have widened the gap in relative growth performance, especially through the recession years of the 1970s. This remarkable growth performance has been noted by others, e.g. Morawetz (1977) who also notes the equally remarkable achievement with regard to broader socio-economic indicators. Table 1.6 sets out some of these indicators and shows that there have been substantial improvements in life expectancy, literacy, education, and so on. Table 1.6 also shows that urban population growth is about twice as large as population growth as a whole. These statistics indicate the extent of rural–urban migration and the associated socio-economic transformation that these changes bring in their wake, see e.g. Sabot (1978). Part of this transformation no doubt includes and complements the achievements in the sphere of economic growth. This theme will be touched on in the chapters ahead.

III Outline of the Book

Methodology

A central assumption is that the economic slowdown in the industrialised countries should be analysed in global terms. To varying degrees the slowdown is a factor common to all

Table 1.6 *Social trends in developing countries 1960–80*

	Low-income countries	Middle-income countries
Life expectancy (years)		
1960	42	53
1979	57	61
Population per doctor		
1960	11680	10430
1977	6150	4380
Adult literacy rate (%)		
1960	28	53
1976	51	72
Primary school enrolment (%)		
1960	76	79
1978	83	95
Crude birth rate per 1000		
1960	40	41
1979	29	34
Crude death rate per 1000		
1960	18	15
1979	11	10
Population growth (% p.a.)		
1960–70	2.2	2.5
1970–9	2.1	2.4
Urban population growth (% p.a.)		
1960–70	3.8	4.1
1970–80	3.7	3.8
Urban population (% of total)		
1960	15	37
1980	17	50

Source: World Bank (1981)

OECD countries; it therefore makes sense to seek explanations that are common to all countries rather than parochial explanations that are specific to each. The parochial methodology implies that the international nature of the slowdown is a coincidence reflecting domestic considerations that vary from country to country. This hardly seems plausible, for the coincidence is too great. This does not imply that parochial factors are irrelevant, but instead that the fundamental causes of the slowdown are global and it is this which establishes the general character of the recession. However, deviations from this general trend may be understood in parochial terms.

This book is almost exclusively concerned with the general trend rather than the aberrations of individual countries. The perspective is therefore top-down rather than bottom-up; the bird's-eye view rather than the worm's-eye view. Inevitably this methodology has its shortcomings and runs the risk of the exceptional case that seems to disprove the general trend. On the other hand, the parochial methodology can miss the wood for the trees.

Chapter 8, however, departs from this general perspective and considers the performance of the UK economy in relation to the global OECD trend. This digression is intended to shed light on the degree to which the protracted recession in the UK over the 1970s can be explained in global terms and the degree to which it is a parochial manifestation of the British Disease.

The centrepiece of this book is the Transition Theory, which argues that an important global factor in the OECD slowdown is the changing balance of world economic power, which has moved in favour of developing countries. Economic expansion in the Third World has threatened the existing economic structures in the OECD countries, which in turn have been slow to adjust to these new circumstances. The origins of the slowdown are therefore structural, in the sense that market forces have changed and economic restructuring is necessary. This classical perspective should be contrasted with the Keynesian view that the economic structure is good but aggregate demand is deficient. The protracted nature of the slowdown is unlikely to be the result of a protracted deficiency of demand, because the time interval of more than ten years should have been long enough for demand and supply to have returned to balance.

Global Theories of Secular Stagnation

Before considering the Transition Theory, existing theories of secular stagnation are reviewed in Chapter 2. Two main hypotheses are reviewed. It is argued by Cornwall (1977) that secular stagnation is an inevitable consequence of the diffusion of technology. The rapid growth in the 1950s and 1960s reflected the exploitation of technologies which for historical reasons, such as war, had not been absorbed previously. As countries caught up with the best technological practice growth was rapid, but as the technological gap was narrowed growth was bound to decelerate. The importance of Cornwall's thesis is not disputed. However, it is argued that this thesis implies a gradual deceleration in secular growth rather than the relatively abrupt transformation between the 1960s and 1970s that actually occurred. Indices of the technological gap are calculated and they show that there were no abrupt breaks in the index between the 1960s and 1970s.

The second hypothesis considered is the one proposed by Bruno and Sachs (1981), that the slowdown has been induced by the rise in the prices of raw materials during the 1970s. According to this theory higher raw materials prices reduce aggregate supply because production costs are raised. They may also have differential effects in the labour and capital markets and in the manufacturing and non-manufacturing sectors of the economy. The Bruno–Sachs thesis undoubtedly provides major insights into the nature of the slowdown from the supply side. However, it assumes that the increase in the price of raw materials is exogenous. While this may be applicable to the OPEC price hikes of 1973–4 it is less plausible to assume that the increase in non-oil raw materials prices some years earlier was exogenous. The sudden transformation in raw materials prices is as curious as the slowdown itself. The Transition Theory attempts to link these phenomena to common third factors.

Chapter 2 digresses to consider the effects of higher oil prices on social welfare. The argument that they were a blessing in disguise, because they warned the world of a pending energy 'crunch', is rejected. At plausible rates of social time preference the sudden increase in oil prices was unjustified and the world was forced to make energy economies at least fifteen years early. This is quite apart from the possibility that pessimistic energy forecasts were in any event wrong.

A related digression is the likely effect upon oil prices of a breakdown in the OPEC cartel. As members go it alone and compete against each other for a limited market the price is likely to crash at a relatively rapid rate. If the cartel broke into two competing groups, consisting of Saudi Arabia on the one hand and the rest of OPEC on the other, the price of oil would be likely to fall by about 40 per cent on the assumption that each group maximises profits.

Since some Western economies have sectors which produce raw materials, Chapter 2 closes with a discussion of the relationship between the price of raw materials, the size of the indigenous raw materials sector and the real exchange rate.

The Transition Theory

The theory is described in Chapter 3 and empirical evidence is brought in Chapter 4. Before describing the theory the existing literature on the economic impact of developing countries on the industralised countries is reviewed. By and large this literature rejects the LDC threat hypothesis. It is argued, however, that these studies are cast in a partial equilibrium setting and their conclusions may break down once the indirect effects of a general equilibrium analysis are brought to bear upon the economic relationships between developed and developing countries. In contrast the Transition Theory is cast in terms of a general economic equilibrium analysis.

The central components of the Transition Theory are as follows:

(1) During the second half of the 1960s there was a sudden spurt in LDC industrialisation that was disproportionately reflected in the manufacturing sector. Clothing, textiles, electronics and a vast range of light manufactures as well as some heavy manufactures benefited from this transition. In the LDCs this was associated with rural–urban transition, as the rural population migrated to the towns in order to take advantage of industrialisation which is essentially urban-based.

The factors behind this transformation are discussed. The most plausible explanation is the more open economic policies that were implemented especially in the so-called 'newly industrialised countries' such as South Korea and Brazil. However, the Transition Theory regards this industrial 'take-off' as a matter of fact, as an autonomous development. It is also noted that the spread of development across the LDCs has not been uniform. On the other hand the aggregation of LDCs simplifies the exposition and mirrors the aggregation of developed countries as already described.

(2) The autonomous increase in the supply of world manufactures from stage 1 began to lower the relative price of manufactures on world markets. The rise in the relative price of raw materials that began towards the end of the 1960s was brought about by supply shocks in the market for manufactures rather than or as much as supply shocks in the market for raw materials.

The fall in the relative price of manufactures provided market signals which caused resources to shift from the manufacturing sector to other sectors of the economy in the bloc of developed countries. This is called the de-industrialisation effect, because industry suffers while the rest of the economy expands.

(3) As de-industrialisation takes place it is likely that the profit share in developed countries falls while the wage share rises. This is because the manufacturing/ industrial sectors of the economy are assumed to be relatively capital intensive, so that a relative contraction of the manufacturing sector results in a fall in the marginal product of capital and an increase in the marginal product of labour.

The market power of capital is thus reduced and the market power of labour as a whole is increased. This was the fundamental cause behind increased trade union power during the late 1960s and the first part of the 1970s. Militancy is circumscribed by market power. It was also the fundamental cause behind the fall in profit rates across the OECD as a whole that began in the late 1960s.

(4) The migration of resources from the manufacturing sector to expanding parts of the economy is not frictionless. Restrictive practices and natural causes of friction imply that economic adjustment in developed countries takes time. During the adjustment, imbalances arise in different sectors of the economy. The

manufacturing sector is recessed while the service and other sectors of the economy are faced with bottle-necks. This mismatch thesis explains the paradox of shortage amidst plenty, since excess supply in the manufacturing/industrial sector may coexist with excess demand in the rest of the economy. Mismatch may be protracted and unemployment is likely to rise while mismatch effects persist. The rise in OECD unemployment that began towards the end of the 1960s may be regarded in part as an implication of the mismatch phenomenon.

(5)   Under Stage 3 the rate of return on capital in developed countries fell. Under Stage 1 autonomous LDC industrialisation tends to raise the rate of return on capital in LDCs. This creates a disequilibrium in the world capital market since a positive differential has opened up in favour of LDCs. This in turn causes capital to move from developed countries to developing countries. As this process takes place LDCs run capital account surpluses and corresponding current account deficits. The current account deficits consist of imports of capital goods that are required to promote the LDC development process. Thus it is the capital account that drives the current account rather than the other way about.

According to the Transition Theory the debt problem of the Third World is therefore an equilibrium rather than a disequilibrium phenomenon, and as such it is not a problem at all. Capital inputs are an essential ingredient and an inevitable consequence of economic development, and in Chapter 4 it is shown that the debt problem began in the late 1960s well before the oil price hikes. Indeed there is no necessary relationship between higher oil import bills and LDC indebtedness. The only necessary relationship is that OPEC surpluses have to equal deficits elsewhere, but that is a different matter that does not depend on whether oil importing countries are developing, centrally planned or industrialised. While the growth of LDC indebtedness as a whole is not a problem this does not imply that in certain cases problems do not exist.

(6)   The Transition Theory implies that a once and for all spurt in LDC industrialisation generates a temporary setback in the developed countries while adjustment takes place. Once the adjustment has occurred, unemployment and growth should approximately return to their original levels. In this sense the theory is about cyclical rather than secular stagnation, but the adjustments may be protracted and this will give rise to a fairly long bout of recession. Mismatch unemployment is inherently temporary, and so the prognosis of the Transition Theory is optimistic. On the other hand, further spurts of development and industrialisation will cause this cycle to be repeated and mismatch effects to accumulate. Since only a small proportion of LDCs have so far been touched by development there is every prospect that further spurts will take place in the decades to come.

The Long Wave

Chapter 5 considers the renewed interest in the Kondratieff long wave as an explanation of the OECD slowdown. According to this theory the slowdown is an inevitable implication of a long wave in economic life which lasts approximately fifty years. Twenty-five fat years ended in 1970 or thereabouts, to be followed by twenty-five lean years which will remain with us until the end of the millennium. Schumpeter's theory of the long wave is compared and contrasted with Rostow's theory. The main argument is that statistical evidence on long waves is too flimsy both in regard to Kondratieff's original data and other time series.

This does not necessarily imply that we are not on course for twenty-five lean years. The central point is that there are no autonomous long waves and the present recession is not inevitable from this point of view. It must be understood in other terms such as the Transition Theory or the various hypotheses explored in Chapter 2. Chapter 5 concludes with a rejection of the Club of Rome thesis that the economic slowdown is an implication of the finite nature of economic resources. According to this view the world has polluted and consumed itself into deeper and deeper secular stagnation.

However, the original proponents of this 'doomwatch' theory did not intend it to apply for at least another fifty years.

The British Economic Climacteric 1870–95

In Chapter 6 it is argued that the British economic climacteric that is purported to have occurred during the latter decades of the nineteenth century is explicable in terms of the Transition Theory. The nineteenth-century precursor to the OECD countries was played by Britain while the latter day developing countries consisted of the US, France, Germany, Russia, Argentina, Australia, etc. These countries challenged the economic supremacy of Britain.

The Great Depression in Britain coincided with economic growth in these newly emerging economies and the parameters of this depression coincided with the deductions of the Transition Theory. Apart from the rise in unemployment, the share of industrial production in GDP was adversely affected and Britain became a substantial capital exporter. In many respects this development was a preview of developments that were to take place a century later. By this time development had spread across what is now the OECD bloc and there is every prospect of history repeating itself.

A re-run of the 1970s

What would have happened to OECD countries had commodity prices behaved as in the 1960s and had oil prices not quadrupled? To answer these questions in Chapter 7 an econometric model of the world economy is deployed which is simulated on the assumption that the commodity and oil price shocks did not occur. We also consider the effects of monetary disturbances and ask how OECD economies would have performed had monetary policy in the 1970s been as stable as it was in the 1960s.

The objective of this exercise is not to cry over spilt milk but to provide orders of magnitude of the gearing of the industrialised economies to the disturbances that actually took place. Since the model does not incorporate Transition

Theory effects, the calculations cannot be related directly to the arguments in Chapters 3, 4 and 6. They are more related to the arguments in Chapter 2.

The Relative Performance of the UK Economy 1950–80

In Chapter 8 the behaviour of the UK economy is compared with the behaviour of the OECD as a whole. Comparisons largely refer to the variables that feature in the Transition Theory. Apart from growth and unemployment, data on profit rates, shares of industrial production in GDP and inflation are examined. The main conclusion is that the UK has weathered the world recession badly. Until 1979 this did not apply to unemployment but it has been especially marked in the case of relative industrial output and the profit rate since the late 1960s. In addition the UK has been more inflation-prone during the 1970s.

The relative position of the UK economy is complicated by the growth of North Sea oil production since 1975 which has 'crowded out' the manufacturing sector through the balance of payments. However, even before this there were signs that the UK had departed from the OECD trend. No attempt has been made to test whether these deviations are explicable in terms of the Transition Theory. However, the greater dependence of the UK economy on manufactures makes it more vulnerable to Transition Theory effects which primarily work through the manufacturing sector.

Policy

The central policy implication of the Transition Theory concerns whether the rich countries should restrict trade and investment relationships with developing countries. To date there have been no attempts to restrict capital flows to developing countries but the same has not applied to trade relationships. The so-called 'new protectionism' has discriminated against developing country exports, and the Multi-Fibre Agreement which was successfully renegotiated at the end of 1981 constitutes a further attempt by the developed countries to limit competition from the Third World.

The Transition Theory implies that LDC industrialisation inflicts a term of trade loss on the developed countries, and in the shorter term it generates mismatch costs. In a narrow sense the theory thus implies that policies designed to thwart LDC economic development are desirable as far as the rich countries are concerned. Despite the economic arguments, politicians seldom base commercial policy on terms of trade considerations and instead regard unemployment as the basis for protectionism. In so far as the Transition Theory implies that unemployment will be temporary this would serve as an argument against protectionism. This would leave as the main political challenge the reduction in man-made frictions which contribute to mismatch effects.

2

Global Theories of Secular Stagnation

Parochial and International Theories

The prevailing trend in economic commentary and research regarding the economic slowdown in the West has been unilateral rather than multilateral. That is, each country is analysed in isolation, usually by its own nationals, and parochial panaceas are proposed in almost complete disregard of the fact that other industrialised countries are beset by broadly similar problems. National parameters are identified as the cause of the malaise. Thus it is argued that public expenditure is sapping economic vitality, high unemployment benefit is increasing voluntary unemployment, the tax system is distorting capital costs in an inflationary environment and depressing investment, trade union reform is necessary, etc., etc. But if, say, public expenditure is to blame in one country, why is it that other countries which seem to be beset by similar difficulties do not have large and growing public sectors? Similar arguments apply to unemployment benefit, trade unionization, and so on.

These national parameters may indeed be important. However, in Chapter 1 it was argued that the recession since the late 1960s has been international in character. Therefore international analyses seem likely to be more fruitful than parochial ones; perhaps the parochial arguments explain deviations from the international trend. The central purpose in this book is, however, to explain the international trend rather than the deviations of particular countries from this trend.

Against this prevailing trend in economic research there

have been three important exceptions which have adopted an international perspective. First, Cornwall (1977) has argued that the economic decline in the West is an inevitable consequence of technology diffusion throughout the industrialised world. There are natural limits to diffusion, which may have been reached, and which imply that the growth performance of the 1950s and 1960s could not last. Secondly, Bruno and Sachs (1981) argue that the rise in the price of raw materials during the 1970s was responsible for the economic slowdown. An extension of their theory covers the effects of the OPEC oil price revolution on economic activity. It was generally recognised at the time that these price developments would trigger recession. Keynesians argued that higher import prices for the OECD as a whole would depress real disposable income and aggregate demand would fall. Monetary economists argued that these higher prices would reduce real financial wealth so that aggregate demand would fall. Most probably both of these recessionary forces were triggered by the price rises. It was also generally thought that the reduction in aggregate demand was temporary and that once wages and domestic prices had adjusted world 'full employment' would prevail once again. The essential insight of Bruno and Sachs is that while the demand side effects may be temporary the supply side effects are permanent and adverse. Therefore normal levels of economic activity never return and the OECD as a whole reaches a new equilibrium in which the capital stock is lower, output is lower and labour productivity is lower than before the price increases.

Both of these global theories of secular stagnation are described fully below. They are global because they apply to varying degrees to all OECD countries and must be contrasted with the parochial theories. All countries have access to technology, all countries consume raw materials and all countries use energy. Therefore the international dimension of the recession must be explained in terms of such global variables.

The third global theory has taken the form of a renaissance of the Kondratieff long wave hypothesis. According to this view the world economy is set for twenty-five lean years after twenty-five fat years that ended around 1970. Once the indulgence of the lunatic fringe, the Kondratieff hypothesis has to some extent become the vogue of the 1970s and 1980s. It is discussed at some length in Chapter 5.

Chapter 3 proposes the Transition Theory as an additional global theory which, however, complements rather than competes with those described in the present chapter.

I Technology

Domestic Diffusion

The relationship between technology and economic growth is complex and numerous commentators have argued that the so-called 'third industrial revolution' based on microelectronics has contributed to the world recession. These and related issues are taken up in greater depth in Chapter 5, where these arguments are rejected. In the meanwhile let us note that economic history suggests the following lessons about industrial revolutions:

(1) Industrial revolutions do not take place overnight. New technologies such as the spinning jenny and electrification diffuse relatively slowly over a generation or even longer.

(2) During this interval labour tends to move from low to high productivity sectors in the economy.

(3) New technologies create new jobs as fast as they destroy old ones. The computer may reduce the need for filing clerks but it also opens up new markets and economic activities. In my own profession erstwhile clerks have become data handlers in the new market for econometric models.

(4) Once the new technologies have been absorbed all elements in society are better off. The generations that benefited from the second industrial revolution in the late nineteenth century are materially better off than the generations that benefited from the first industrial revolution a century before. We have every reason to expect that the generations that benefit from the third industrial revolution of the second half of the twentieth century will be better off than ourselves.

(5) However, while new technologies are being absorbed there will be economic casualties and human tragedy. This is especially true of older employees who find it difficult to retrain. This will generate Luddite tendencies and perhaps political tensions. It should not be beyond the limits of social policy to ensure that these casualties are recompensed out of the profits of society as a whole.

(6) Before the event each industrial revolution is forecast as a socio-economic disaster; such is the pessimism of man.

To illustrate these lessons, let us use an econometric simulation of domestic technological diffusion of the microchip which is based on the analysis of Beenstock (1979). Barron and Curnow (1979) have estimated that the labour deplacement effect in the UK caused by the diffusion of microprocessors will be in the region of 16 per cent. This means that the introduction of microprocessors will enable the same volume of output to be produced with a labour force that is 16 per cent smaller. They stress, however, that the labour deplacement effect is likely to be the strongest in the case of office staff and clerical workers. Barron and Curnow in common with many other commentators take the pessimistic view that this will most probably cause unemployment to rise by 10 to 15 percentage points.

But this argument cannot be right, for it is tantamount to arguing that the industrial revolution of 200 years ago with its presumed labour deplacement effects has kept unemployment up for the last two centuries. Unemployment may rise in the short term but in the longer term employment may actually rise rather than fall. The transmission mechanism between technology and employment involves adjustments in the labour and product markets. To explore this transmission mechanism further, the aggregate labour market model reported by Beenstock and Warburton (1982) is deployed. According to this model a reduction in the demand for labour causes real wage rates to fall because of excess supply in the labour market. The fall in real wages makes labour competitive relative to capital and the demand for labour recovers.

The supply of labour in the model varies directly with real wages rates, i.e. higher wage rates create positive work incentives so that the supply of labour rises. The demand for labour also depends on the level of economic activity which, in the present context, is increased by the new markets that microprocessors open up. These are the job creation effects.

It is assumed that the 16 per cent labour displacement effect is distributed over 16 years since, as noted above, technological change does not occur overnight. The job creation effects are distributed over a similar time period but with a two-year lag behind the displacement effect. The lag reflects the existence of a two-year gestation period between the absorption of new technology and the development of new products.

Figure 2.1 shows the employment effects generated through the model on the basis of the above assumptions. Initially employment falls by 1 per cent and continues to fall until the job creation effect begins to take place. In addition by years 2–3 real wages decline with excess labour supply so that labour becomes more competitive. These two effects cause employment to recover so that by year 13 the net change in employment is zero. Figure 2.1 shows that employment rises eventually by $\frac{1}{2}$ per cent. This reflects the

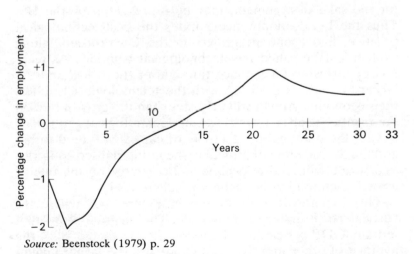

Source: Beenstock (1979) p. 29

Figure 2.1   *Employment effects of microprocessors*

increase in the productivity of labour caused by the microprocessors and the associated rise in real wage rates by 4 per
cent. Higher real wage rates increase the supply of labour
which, because of the low elasticities in the model, only raise
labour supply by $\frac{1}{2}$ per cent.

Therefore the results of this simulation accord with the six
lessons listed on pp. 23–4 including Number 6. On this basis
it can be concluded that the labour market disruption generated by the diffusion of microprocessors is unlikely to be
very serious.

International Diffusion

Thus far the focus has been on the diffusion of technology
within a given country. We now return to our main subject
matter which is the international dimension of the economic
slowdown in the West.

Cornwall (1977) proposes an appealing hypothesis about
the deceleration of economic growth. His basic hypothesis is
that as technological know-how becomes diffused throughout the world, income levels will be higher but economic
growth will slow down. His theory begins with the assumption that for various reasons and to different degrees individual countries lag behind the technological leader which,
for the sake of argument, may be represented by the US.
Thus the US economy incorporates the best technological
practice, and economic growth in the US proceeds along
what might be called the 'technological frontier'. As technology diffusion takes place throughout the world and the
laggard countries catch up with the technological frontier,
their economic growth will be faster than the growth rate on
the frontier itself. However, as the technological gap is narrowed, the marginal productivity of capital will tend to fall
and the average rate of growth in the industrialised countries
as a whole will tend to decline and converge on the rate of
growth dictated by the technological frontier.

This hypothesis is illustrated in Figure 2.2, where the
vertical axis is drawn on a log scale. The diagram shows that
initially GDP per capita is higher in the US than it is for the
average of other industrialised countries, the laggard countries. The diagram shows that technology does not stand

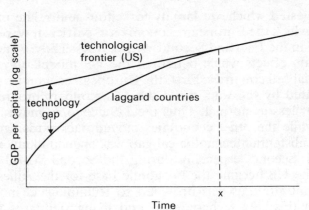

Source: private calculations based on UN sources

Figure 2.2 *Technology diffusion and growth*

still since economic growth continues to take place along the technological frontier. The essence of the diffusion hypothesis is that GDP per capita in the laggard countries is lower because they have as yet not incorporated the best technological practice. Over time and in the absence of any constraints on the international transfer of technology the laggard countries may narrow the technology gap by investing in better technology. As they do economic growth in the laggard countries proceeds faster than in the US. However, as the technology gap is narrowed and the best options are used up, growth in the laggard countries tends to decelerate. It becomes increasingly difficult to find good investment opportunities and profitability falls. Eventually a point in time is reached (x) when the technology gap is eliminated completely and individual growth rates tend to converge upon the growth rate dictated by the technological frontier. At this point the technological complexions of the various industrialised countries appear quite similar.

This hypothesis implies that in the industrialised countries as a whole the average rate of economic growth would have a secular tendency to fall and it is arguable that this partly explains the slower growth rates that have been observed. However, to complete the theory it is necessary to explain why a technological gap existed in the first place. If we take the late 1940s as our starting point a number of reasons may be suggested which are largely fortuitous and relate to the way in which the European economies in particular were embroiled in the First and Second World Wars. These wars had two main effects which benefited the US relative to other industrialised countries. First, the European economies were devastated by the wars while the US economy progressed more or less as normal. Thus the US economy moved forward while the other economies moved backwards. In this way a substantial technological gap was opened in favour of the US. Second, especially during the Second World War when the US became the economic base for the Allies, an important stimulus was provided to technological innovation. In this way technological and living standards were considerably higher in the US by the late 1940s.

Using pooled cross section and time series data, Cornwall (p. 142) reports the following regression equation for the rate of growth of manufacturing output:

$$\dot{Q}m = -0.036 + 0.953(q_{us}/q) + 0.229(I/Q)m \quad \bar{R}^2 = 0.8$$
$$\phantom{\dot{Q}m = -0.036 +} (0.286) \phantom{(q_{us}/q) +} (0.083)$$

where

$\dot{Q}m$ is the annual rate of growth of manufacturing output

q is GDP per capita

q_{us} is GDP per capita in the US

$(I/Q)m$ is the ratio of investment to value added in manufacturing.

Standard errors are reported in parentheses.

Cornwall's equation implies that for each 1 per cent increase in the investment ratio output growth rises by 0.229 per cent. It also implies that when the technology gap falls by 10 percentage points (as measured by the ratio of GDP per capita in the US relative to the GDP per capita of the country in question) the rate of growth of manufacturing output falls by 0.953 per cent. The equation implies a geometric rate of convergence upon the technological frontier.

Figure 2.3 below indicates that in 1950 GDP per capita in the US was on average 160 per cent greater than elsewhere in the OECD. Assuming a constant investment ratio, Cornwall's equation implies that in 1950 the technology gap accounted for manufacturing growth of 2.48 per cent per year. This growth reduced the gap so that in the next year the gap must contribute a smaller amount of catch-up growth. The dynamics of the model imply that the catch-up growth falls by 0.06 per cent per year, i.e. 2.48 per cent, 2.42 per cent, 2.36 per cent etc. On this basis it would take forty-one years for other countries to reach the technological frontier. In terms of Figure 2.2, x is forty-one years away from the origin. During the first ten years the gap falls from 160 per cent to 109 per cent, during the next ten it falls to 77 per cent. These theoretical declines are smaller than the actual declines recorded on Figure 2.3 where by 1977 the gap had narrowed from 160 per cent in 1950 to approximately 25 per cent.

The diffusion theory represents an important insight, which no doubt underpins the history of economic growth in the world economy since the last war. However, it does not lend itself to the sudden deceleration in growth that occurred in the late 1960s. To have done so it would be necessary that the technological gap suddenly narrowed around the same time, yet this did not happen. Instead, as Figure 2.3 shows, the average technological gap fell more or less steadily from 1950. Nevertheless, between 1965 and 1970 there was some

Figure 2.3 *Index of technological gap 1950–77*

acceleration in the rate at which the gap was narrowed, although this could hardly have been responsible for the change in economic growth around that time.

The index that is measured on the vertical axis of Figure 2.3 is:

$$D = \sum_{i=1}^{10} w_{it}(q_{us}/q_i)_t - 1$$

where w_i represents the GDP share of the i'th country. (The ten countries were Canada, Austria, France, West Germany, Italy, Netherlands, Sweden, Switzerland, UK and Japan.) Thus like Cornwall we assume the US economy lies on the technological frontier. The index approaches zero when the gap is completely closed. By 1977 this had been greatly narrowed to around 25 per cent. This is not the place to comment on the performances of individual countries although Stout (1979) analyses the relatively poor performance of the UK economy. For a variety of reasons technology has failed to diffuse into the UK as it has done in other industrialised countries so that the marginal productivity of capital has been relatively low. On the other, this implies that the potential for growth in the UK is high since it has relatively more catching up to do.

II   Raw Materials

This section describes the general contributions of Bruno and Sachs (1979, 1981) which are concerned with the structural effects of the price of imported raw materials upon the supply side of the economy. It then goes on to consider the special effects arising from an increase in energy prices. Finally, it departs from the main topic of the international character of the slowdown by considering the special problems of energy-producing OECD countries.

The Bruno–Sachs Model

The essence of the Bruno–Sachs analysis may be demonstrated with a very simple model of the economy. We begin by postulating an economy with an aggregate production function for gross output (Q) which depends on inputs of capital services (K), employment (L) and raw materials (R):

$$Q = F(K, L, R)$$

Positive but diminishing returns are assumed to apply to each factor of production. For simplicity, we assume that the economy does not have a raw materials sector of its own so that R must be entirely imported. The price of output is P and the price of raw materials is represented by P_R. Hence real income (Y) is given by:

$$Y = Q - RP_R/P$$

When the relative price of raw materials rises the terms of trade deteriorate and real disposable income declines.

Entrepreneurs are assumed to maximise their profits, which are given by:

$$\pi = Q - wL - cK - P_R^* R$$

where w is the own product real wage (i.e. the nominal wage rate relative to the price of output as opposed to the general price level), c is the cost of capital analogously defined and $P_R^* = P_R/P$. Maximising π subject to the production function generates the following first order conditions:

$$F'_k(K, L, R) = c$$
$$F'_L(K, L, R) = w$$
$$F'_R(K, L, R) = P_R^*$$

which solve for the equilibrium values of K, L and R in terms of c, w and P_R^*. The cost of capital is assumed to be fixed because either it reflects the rate of time preference (which is approximately independent of the variables under consideration) or it reflects world interest rates which are assumed to be given. Likewise the real cost of raw materials is determined exogenously. If the supply of labour is inelastic about $\bar{L}$ the model may be solved for the real wage rate rather than the other way round.

A *ceteris paribus* rise in the real price of raw materials will reduce entrepreneurs' demand for raw materials, just in the same way that an autonomous rise in the wage rate would reduce the demand for labour. The rise in P_R^* causes the marginal product of raw materials to fall below their marginal cost. To bring this marginal product back into line with the new price it is necessary to reduce the level of R. The fall in R will tend to lower marginal labour and capital products through the production function. This in turn will generate disequilibrium conditions in the labour and capital markets.

Before taking this analysis any further on Figure 2.4 we present the factor price frontier that is implied by these simple theoretical constructs. We assume that the real price of raw materials is P_{R1}^* so that the optimal level of raw materials is R_1. The curve $F(P_{R1}^*)$ describes the relationships between marginal labour and capital products when capital and labour are efficiently combined with R_1. At a these marginal products are respectively c_1 and w_1, while labour productivity is given by x and capital productivity by y. The slope of the factor–price frontier measures the capital–labour ratio.

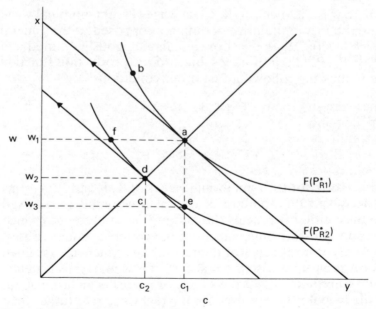

Figure 2.4 *The factor–price frontier*

At b the capital–labour ratio is higher so that both the average and marginal products of labour are higher while the opposite applies in the case of capital. The factor price frontier is convex to the origin because of the usual assumptions about diminishing marginal rates of substitution between capital and labour in the production function.

As argued above, profit maximisation implies that a rise in the price of raw materials to P_{R2}^* causes the demand for raw materials to contract. This means that if capital and labour remain at their initial levels of K_1 and L_1 their marginal products will be lower. This in turn implies that the factor price frontier has shifted towards the origin. In Figure 2.4 the new factor price frontier is represented by $F(P_{R2}^*)$. At d the capital–labour ratio is the same as at a (because the slopes of the tangents are the same) and the marginal labour product has fallen to w_2 and the marginal capital product has fallen to c_2. Hence d is a partial equilibrium solution in which $K = K_1$, $L = L_1$ and $R = R_2$. Because R_2 is less than R_1 the production function implies that output has fallen.

Thus far it can be concluded that the partial equilibrium effects of a rise in the price of raw materials are:

- a decline in the consumption of raw materials,
- a decline in the marginal and average products of labour and capital, and
- a fall in the level of output.

These are supply side effects, which are quite independent of any demand side effects brought about through the erosion of wealth positions, etc.

If real wages fall to w_2 and the cost of capital fell to c_2, d would represent a general equilibrium solution too. If, however, the cost of capital is exogenously fixed at c_1, the general equilibrium solution is at e, where reductions in the capital stock have raised the marginal product of capital back in line with the cost of capital. This reduction in the capital–labour ratio implies a further fall in the equilibrium real wage to w_3. This implies that for the level of employment to remain at L_1 the real wage rate must fall from w_1 to w_3. If L_1 represents full employment and real wages do not fall to w_3, the demand for labour will fall and unemployment will rise. In addition the lower level of employment will result in a fall in output.

Hence the general equilibrium effects of a rise in the price of raw materials are:

● a decline in the consumption of raw materials,
● a fall in the capital labour ratio leading to a fall in investment,
● the real wage falls for two reasons, because R is lower and because K is lower, and
● output falls for these two reasons too.

If, however, real wages are sticky and do not fall to w_3 there will be two further effects:

● unemployment and
● further declines in output in line with the fall in employment.

The intuitive reason for the decline in own product real wages is that the higher cost of raw materials reduces profits and entrepreneurs respond by raising their own prices (P) relative to other input costs. This argument has been recognised by most economic commentators, who have also recognised that the deterioration in the terms of trade associated with the higher real cost of imported raw materials means that real wages would in any event have to fall. What is less well-known is the real wage reduction necessitated by the fall in the capital stock. Hence real wages fall for three reasons:

● Own product real wages fall as entrepreneurs raise prices to restore profit margins.
● The terms of trade loss is reflected in lower wage rates.
● As the capital stock falls, productivity falls and thus real wages fall.

Table 2.1 bears out some but not all of the Bruno–Sachs predictions.

The price of intermediate products largely reflects the price of imported raw materials. Having declined on average

Table 2.1 *Rates of growth in the manufacturing sector 1955–78 (% p.a.)*

	Labour productivity	Capital– labour ratio	Price of intermediate products (P_R^*)	Own product real wages
1955–72	5.2	4.0	−0.5	5.9
1972–8	3.4	4.1	2.4[a]	2.7

Source: Bruno (1981) Table 1: averages for US, UK, West Germany and Japan
Note: a. 1955–71, 1971–8

by 0.5 per cent per annum up to 1972 they rose thereafter with the explosion of commodity prices in the early 1970s and the OPEC oil price hikes of 1973–74. The growth of labour productivity declined as expected as did own product real wages. Bruno's regression results (p. 30) suggest that given the capital–labour ratio, a 1 per cent rise in P_R^* reduces labour productivity by 0.179 per cent. On this basis the change in the growth of P_R^* shown in Table 2.1 should have brought about a reduction in productivity growth of 0.52 per cent. In fact the reduction was 1.8 per cent.

Table 2.1 does not indicate any fall in the rate of growth of the capital–labour ratio. The measurement problems in this area are very considerable and it is possible that the capital stock figures are overestimated. The fact remains that for the industrialised countries as a whole the rate of growth of gross domestic fixed capital formation fell from 5.6 per cent per annum in the 1960s to 1.4 per cent per annum in the 1970s. In addition, the relative price changes of the 1970s most probably caused an acceleration in capital obsolescence. Therefore, in all probability the capital–labour ratio has declined.

De-Industrialisation

By de-industrialisation we refer to falls in the share of industrial output in total output. Hence a rapidly growing economy may also experience industrial growth, but if the industrial production ratio is declining we shall say that it is de-industrialising. Perhaps this relative definition does not necessarily conjure images of industrial decay but at least

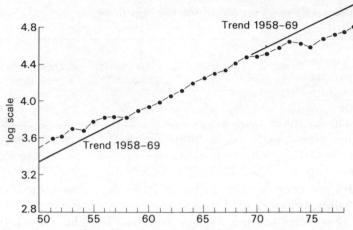

Source: *Statistical Yearbook* (New York: UN) various issues

Figure 2.5 *The ratio of industrial activity to GDP in developed market economies 1950–78*

it can be measured. Another advantage is that it relates directly to the phenomenon noted in Chapter 1: that recession has affected the industrial sector to a disproportionate extent. During the 1970s GDP growth in industrialised countries fell by 37 per cent relative to the 1960s. The comparable figures for industrial production and manufacturing were 48 per cent and 52 per cent.

Figure 2.5 shows the behaviour of this index over the postwar period. During the 1950s the index rose almost imperceptibly. During the 1960s it rose more convincingly, especially after 1963. Peak to peak measures in the trend of the index show that around 1970 the index began to falter and de-industrialisation emerged during the 1970s.

The Bruno–Sachs model may be extended to shed light on this phenomenon, which happens to coincide with the revolution in raw materials prices. Thus far a single sector model has been assumed. We now assume that there are two sectors, producing industrial (Q_1) and non-industrial (Q_2) output respectively. These sectors approximately correspond with those for traded and non-traded goods.

We may write the respective production functions as

$$Q_1 = F_1(L_1, K_1, R_1, Q_{21})$$
$$Q_2 = F_2(L_2, K_2, R_2, Q_{12})$$

This specification assumes that each product serves as both a final and an intermediate product, since Q_{21} denotes the input of non-industrial output in the production of industrial goods and Q_{12} denotes the input of industrial output in the production of non-industrial goods. Firms are assumed to maximise profits as before. The labour and capital markets are assumed to be homogeneous in the sense that wage rates and capital costs are the same in both sectors. If, for example, entrepreneurs in the industrial sector paid higher wage rates than in the non-industrial sector this would create a mass exodus of the workers from the latter to the former until wage rates had been equalised once more. The same principles are assumed to apply in the capital market.

If Q_1 is traded internationally and markets are perfectly competitive P_1 will be exogenous, since it is determined in the world market. Alternatively the demand for Q_1 may be elastic. For the present, however, the concern is with the relative price of industrial production $(P_1/P_2 = P_1^*)$ and its relationship with the relative supply of industrial production Q_1/Q_2 which is our de-industrialisation index.

As before, the factor price frontiers for the two sectors can be derived. Unless the techniques are identical these frontiers will have different shapes and will respond differently to shocks. To make our story more interesting, we make the following assumptions:

(1) Industrial production is relatively dependent on raw materials.

(2) Domestic value added in the industrial sector is capital intensive (relative to the non-industrial sector).

On Figure 2.6 the industrial factor price frontier is initially represented by the curve A, and the initial equilibrium is assumed to be at a. Hence c^* denotes the exogenously-given cost of capital. The initial factor price frontier for the non-industrial sector is represented by the curve B. Because factor markets are assumed to be homogeneous this curve must intersect A at a, otherwise factor prices would not be equalised between sectors.

The relationship between the own product wage rates is:

$$W_2 = W_1/P_1^*$$

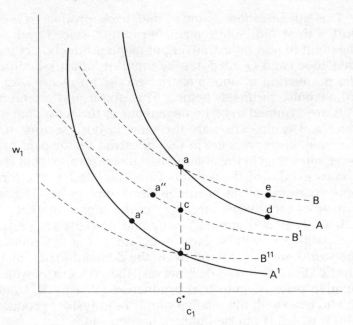

Figure 2.6   *De-industrialisation and raw materials*

Hence a rise in the relative price of industrial output (P_1^*) reduces the own product real wage in the non-industrial sector when measured in units of W_1. In terms of Figure 2.6, a rise in P_1^* would therefore cause the non-industrial factor price frontier to contract towards the origin.

Since the slope of the tangent measures the capital–labour ratio, Figure 2.6 implies that at a industrial production is capital intensive in accordance with assumption (2). Thus if the cost of capital were to rise above c^* the new partial equilibria would diverge to, say, d and e. This implies that real wages must fall in both sectors, but the fall in the industrial sector is larger because of its capital intensity. The story cannot, of course, end here because wage rates cannot diverge. If non-industrial labour earned higher wages than industrial labour, workers would shift out of the industrial sector. This would induce a relative decline in industrial output which would in turn cause the relative price of industrial output to rise. The rise in P_1^* would cause the non-industrial factor price schedule to contract towards the origin. The contraction would continue until B intersected A at d at some higher relative price of industrial production.

The reduction in the capital stock thus has two de-industrialising effects:

(1) Because of the greater capital intensity of industrial value added, a reduction in the capital stock dispropor-tionately affects the industrial sector.

(2) Labour will shift out of the industrial sector since non-industrial employers can afford to pay higher wages.

Using this framework, let us now consider the effects of an increase in the real price of raw materials. Assumption 1 above implies that when profits are maximised the contrac-tion in the industrial factor price frontier will be greater than the contraction in the non-industrial factor price frontier. Hence curve A moves to A', and curve B moves to B'. At a' the industrial capital–labour ratio is the same as at a and at a'' the non-industrial capital–labour ratio is the same as at a. The rise in P_R^* reduces R_1 by more than it does R_2, in which case marginal labour and capital products will fall to a greater degree in the industrial sector at the initial capital–labour ratio. It is for this reason that curve A contracts more than curve B.

Assuming the cost of capital and associated interest rates do not alter, the new partial equilibrium will be at b in the industrial sector and at c in the non-industrial sector. At this partial equilibrium the fall in Q_1 will be larger than the fall in Q_2, for two reasons:

(1) the fall in R_1 is greater than the fall in R_2

(2) the fall in the capital stock that is necessary to bring the marginal product of capital back into line with the cost of capital affects industrial value added to a greater degree, because it is more capital intensive.

Because non-industrial wages are higher at c than at b labour will shift out of the industrial sector into the non-industrial sector. In general equilibrium this will cause the relative price of industrial production to rise and the non-industrial factor price frontier will contract until it intersects curve A' at b. Therefore the general equilibrium non-industrial factor price frontier is represented by curve B". This produces a third cause of de-industrialisation:

(3)   the latent rise in relative non-industrial wages causes labour to shift from the industrial to the non-industrial sector.

This discussion begs two questions. Is industrial output more dependent on raw materials than output as a whole? Is domestic value added in the industrial sector capital intensive? Intuition suggests an affirmative answer in both cases, since tertiary production (services, etc.) seems to be largely generated by labour. This is only a hunch and cetainly is not intended as a substitute for research. But it is not an issue that will be investigated here in view of the formidable data problems on an international scale. Nevertheless as an explanation of de-industrialisation the above analysis is compelling.

Thus far we have assumed that the economy does not have its own raw materials sector. This has largely reflected analytical convenience, although it may not be too far off the mark. In certain cases, however, the approximation may be too crude. For example, the US and UK have sizeable energy sectors. It should be obvious that an increase in the price of raw materials will draw resources into the production of raw materials to the detriment of other sectors of the economy. This is bound to reduce the relative size of the manufacturing sector.

Energy

Most of the discussion so far applies to energy as an example of a raw material. Therefore despite its importance relatively little will be said about the energy price revolution which should have generated all the recessionary and de-industrialising effects discussed so far.

Figure 2.7 plots the behaviour of OPEC oil prices in real terms. A feature of this figure is that it is not given in constant dollars, because fluctuations in the dollar exchange rate will distort the index. It is instead based on the 'effec-

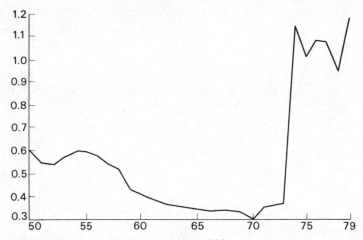

Source: Beenstock and Willcocks (1981) p. 229

Figure 2.7   *The real oil price 1950–79 (1975 = 1.0)*

tive' exchange rate index which essentially internationalises
the real oil price in an appropriate way. The characteristics
of Figure 2.7 are depressingly familiar. Real oil prices
declined gradually in the 1950s and 1960s. They ceased to
do so at the end of the 1960s. The exercise of OPEC's cartel
powers almost quadrupled oil prices in 1973–4 but they
began to slip back until the Iranian Revolution and associated oil supply reductions afforded OPEC the opportunity
of raising them once more in 1978–9.

The OPEC pricing cartel formally broke down in
December 1979 when delegates could not agree on uniform
prices and members decided to go it alone. At the time this
did not matter, because the oil market was tight. At OPEC's
meeting in August 1981 members continued to fail to settle
their differences. At the time of writing, real oil prices
remain at their present levels. A glut in the oil market could
cause world oil prices to crash as each member competed for
a contracting market. By March 1982 the cartel was facing
its greatest crisis since 1973, and Saudi Arabia announced
that to defend the price of oil it was prepared to reduce its
production to $7\frac{1}{2}$ million barrels a day, which was 25 per cent
below the production level of only two years previously. The
pressure on the cartel is reflected in Figures 2.9 and 2.10.

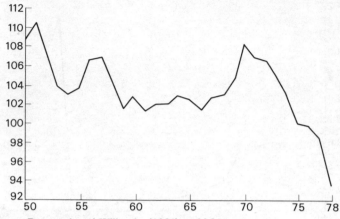

Source: Beenstock and Willcocks (1981) p. 226

Figure 2.8   *The ratio of total energy consumption to GDP in developed market economies 1950–78 (1975 = 100)*

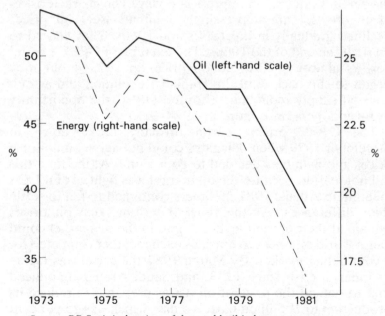

Source: BP Statistical review of the world oil industry

Figure 2.9   *OPEC market shares 1973–81*

Between 1965 and 1973 OPEC oil production grew at an average annual rate of 10.2 per cent. Figure 2.8 reveals that the OPEC price hikes stopped this growth in its tracks and that between 1973 and 1979 there was no growth at all. Since 1979, however, OPEC oil production has fallen sharply and in January 1982 it was 31 per cent below its average level for 1979.

OPEC's share of the world oil and energy markets has declined rapidly as Figure 2.9 reveals. By the end of 1981 its share of the oil market had fallen by about a third, and its share of the energy market had fallen by 40 per cent relative to 1973 levels. Moreover, the rate at which it has been losing its market share has been accelerating. If these trends continue, OPEC will become a residual supplier in the near future and will no longer be able to control world oil prices. It is difficult to believe that OPEC would have survived thus far but for the reduction in Iranian oil production of 5 million barrels per day as a result of the fall of the Shah.

It is worth considering what the effects of a crack in the cartel might be. More specifically, how would oil prices behave as members went it alone in an optimal way, i.e. by maximising their profits at each other's expense? Let us consider what might happen if OPEC split into two competing cartels, or three, or more, and so on until all members are in complete competition with one another.

We apply Cournot's theory of oligopolistic equilibrium (instead of mineral water wells as in Cournot's original case we have oil wells). Cournot showed that the price declines exponentially with the number of producers towards marginal cost. As the number of competing producers approaches infinity, price approaches marginal cost. It is assumed that there are N producers. For the nth producer net revenue (R) from oil production would be:

$$R_n = (P - C)Q_n$$

where

$$P = \text{price of oil}$$

$$C = \text{marginal production costs}$$

$$Q_n = \text{oil production/sales}$$

Each producer is assumed to choose that rate of sales which maximises his net revenue given his competitors' rate of sales. Differentiating the expression for net revenue with respect to Q_n and setting the result to zero yields:

$$\frac{\partial R_n}{\partial Q_n} = P - C - \chi Q_n = 0$$

where $\chi = dP/dQ$ is the marginal response of the price to aggregate supply. Summing the above result for all producers gives:

$$N(P - C) - \chi Q = 0$$

which implies:

$$\frac{\partial Q}{\partial N} = \frac{P - C}{2\chi}$$

Substituting for $\chi = dP/dQ$, this expression implies that the relationship between the price of oil and the number of competing producers is:

$$\frac{\partial P}{\partial N} = \frac{C - P}{2}$$

the solution of which is:

$$P = Ae^{N/2} + C$$

where A and C are constraints.

When OPEC is united, $N = 1$. If for argument's sake OPEC quadrupled the oil price relative to costs, i.e. when $N = 1$ $P = 4C$, it follows that:

$$A = (4 - 1)e^{1/2} = 4.946$$

Table 2.2 shows how the oil price collapses when OPEC disintegrates. If, say, OPEC were to split into three competing groups, prices would fall by about a half. Hence prices

Table 2.2 *Oil prices and OPEC disintegration*

	Number of groups into which OPEC splits			
	---	---	---	---
	2	3	4	5
Percentage price fall	29.5	47.75	58.5	64.75

would fall from about \$35 per barrel to around \$15 per barrel at 1981 prices. These calculations assume that the groups are of equal size, which ignores the predominant role of Saudi Arabia. Nevertheless, the calculations are useful in showing the broad orders of magnitude of the price collapse that might be brought about by dissension within OPEC. The price is very sensitive to disunity.

It is arguable that but for the Iranian Revolution OPEC might have cracked and this crash would already have occurred. Indeed, by the first half of 1978 the real price of oil had fallen by about 30 per cent from its peak in 1974. The scene was set for a collapse. Despite the 'doomwatch' predictions of an energy 'crunch' in the late 1990s (see Chapter 5), a collapse of oil prices should be regarded as a plausible scenario, along with other scenarios, for the 1980s.

One final point on the subject of oil prices is that OPEC's behaviour has been anti-social. In 1970 nobody argued that oil prices would have to be quadrupled on the grounds of depletion policy. In many quarters, however, it was thought that oil prices might harden to some extent, but this is an entirely different matter. But by the late 1970s it was commonly argued that the oil price revolution was indeed a blessing in disguise, because it warned the world that an energy shortage was on the horizon. There was no justification for this sudden change of mind. If indeed energy was likely to be in short supply at some date in the future, and prices were going to quadruple (for argument's sake) by 2000, the socially optimal pricing formula would be:

$$P(t) = P^* e^{-\delta(2000-t)}$$

where P^* is the price in 2000 and δ is the rate of discount. Table 2.3 indicates the socially optimal oil price rise in 1974 under different assumptions about the discount rate. Assum-

Table 2.3   *The socially optimal oil price rise in 1974*

Oil price rise (%)	Discount rate (% p.a.)
210	$2\frac{1}{2}$
112	5
34	10

ing a quadrupling of oil prices was eventually justified, Table 2.3 shows that there was no social basis for OPEC's behaviour in 1974, or for that matter in 1978–9. The world has been forced to conserve energy and develop new energy sources without any social justification. At the same time OPEC, as well as free-riders such as the UK, Mexico, etc., have been reaping monopoly profits that have no social justification.

Although real oil prices have approximately quadrupled since 1973, real energy prices to final users have barely doubled. This reflects the imperfect substitutability between oil and other forms of primary energy, specific rather than *ad valorem* duties on imported oil, and government interference in energy pricing in the consuming countries. Table 2.4 underlines the point that the upshot of these has been to distort yet further the price of energy to different users. Industry has been the hardest hit, while transport has come off rather lightly. A rational price response would have been the same proportionate increase in all sectors.

Figure 2.10 shows that the price hikes have had a dramatic effect on energy productivity, which rose by about 12 per cent between 1973 and 1980. Moreover, the chart indicates

Table 2.4   *Real energy prices to final users in major industrial market economies 1973–80 (1973 = 100)*

User	1973	1974	1976	1978	1979	1980
Residential and commercial	100	123	138	146	168	178
Industry	100	130	160	170	185	274
Transport	100	122	119	111	131	156
TOTAL	100	125	140	144	162	195

Source: Economic Outlook (Paris: OECD) 1981

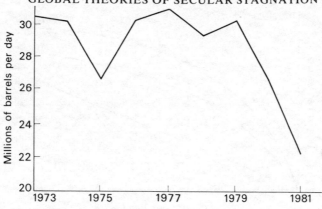

Source: *Petroleum Economist*

Figure 2.10   *OPEC oil production 1973–81*

that further improvements are likely. The rapid rise in user prices between 1978 and 1980 (see Table 2.4) implies that further conservation can be expected, while the full conservation effects of the original price hikes of 1973–4 have yet to come through.

As argued above, a rise in the price of raw materials permanently depresses aggregate supply. Econometric results reported at length in Chapters 4 and 7 suggest that a quadrupling of the real oil price has the following long term effects on output:

- output as a whole falls by 2 per cent, but
- manufacturing output in OECD countries falls by about 12 per cent.

This relative decline in manufacturing supports the de-industrialisation analysis described above. Notice that both here and in the more general case of movements in raw materials prices the rate of growth is not permanently affected; it is only the level of output that is affected. Of course, if raw materials prices grew in real terms the economic growth rate would be affected. However, the basic relationship is between levels of output and levels of raw materials prices and not rates of growth of output and levels of raw materials prices.

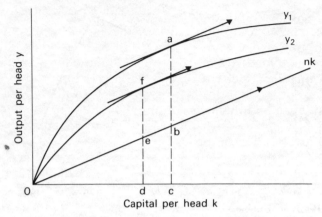

Figure 2.11   *Energy and the golden rule of economic growth*

This result is intuitively enough understood because the determinants of optimal growth paths will be unaltered. The golden rule of economic growth states that the rate of growth (g) depends on the rate of population growth (n), the rate of depreciation (δ) and the rate of technical progress (λ):

$$g = n + \lambda - \delta$$

If higher raw materials prices affect n, λ or δ, the long-run growth rate will be affected. But it is difficult to invent reasons why these parameters should vary. This story is told on Figure 2.11 where Oy_1 plots the relationship between per capita output (y) and the capital–labour ratio for given raw materials prices. Assuming the production future is weakly separable with respect to raw materials (i.e. the ratio of the marginal labour and capital products is not affected by the volume of raw materials; in terms of Figure 2.4 weak separability implies that the tangent at f is parallel to the tangent at a), the tangent of Oy measures the marginal product of capital. At a the marginal product of capital is equal to the saving ratio required to maintain the capital–labour ratio at c. At c consumption is maximised because investment per capita is equal to cb while consumption is equal to ab. If k were higher than c, per capita income would be higher but consumption would be lower on account of the higher savings required to sustain the higher value of k. Consumption would also be lower if k were less than c.

Thus the golden rule for any society is to choose a capital–labour ratio which maximises the level of consumption. If the rate of population growth were to rise, the Onk line would steepen and the new optimum would be to the left of a, implying a higher marginal product of capital and a lower optimal level of consumption.

The rise in the price of raw materials has two effects on Oy. First, as the consumption of raw materials falls, Oy will fall to Oy_2. Secondly, Figure 2.4 implies that k will fall, say, from c to d, in which case the slope of Oy_2 will equal nk at f. The golden rule implies that output has fallen from ac to fd, investment has fallen from bc to ed, and consumption from ab to fe. However, the optimal growth rate remains what it was before the change in raw materials prices, because the growth parameters (n, δ and λ) are unchanged.

Yet the 1970s create the impression that it is the rate of growth of output that has suffered permanently, which suggests that our theorising so far has been wrong. On the other hand, the transition from one optimal path to another could create the impression that the rate of growth has fallen permanently, as illustrated in Figure 2.12. At t_0 the price

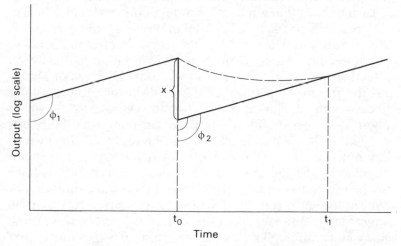

Figure 2.12 *Temporary slow growth and raw materials prices*

of raw materials is assumed to rise. The permanent fall in output is x, and because $\phi_1 = \phi_2$ the growth rate is not affected by the increase in the price of raw materials. Just before t_0 the economy is presumed to be on its optimal growth path. It may, however, be some time before the new optimum is achieved, because entrepreneurs cannot adjust instantaneously to new price relativities. In Figure 2.12 we assume the adjustment period is t_0t_1, and the dotted line shows the actual path of output. Over this period it looks as if the growth rate has slowed down but the diagram indicates that this is only a temporary phenomenon.

Before concluding the discussion of the relationship between energy and output it is worth reporting the results of the empirical analysis of Berndt and Wood (1979). They argue that the evidence suggests that the aggregate production function, where energy (E) is a factor of production, is weakly separable with respect to employment; i.e. the production function takes the form:

$$Q = F\{G(K,E),L\}$$

This means that energy and capital combine in the usual way to produce a flow of productive services (G) which then combine with labour to generate output. Therefore labour competes with G but not with capital and energy separately. This in turn implies that a fall in L produces proportionate falls in the marginal products of capital and energy when K and E are at their initial levels. Alternatively, it implies that a fall in E causes the marginal product of capital to fall without affecting the marginal product of labour. In terms of Figure 2.4 the rise in the price of energy and the subsequent fall in E causes the factor price frontier to contract as shown in Figure 2.13. The points a, e and d correspond with the points a, e and d shown on Figure 2.4. On Figure 2.13, however, d lies horizontally to the left of a, i.e. the real wage is not affected by the fall in E. Instead, all the adjustment is born by the return to capital. This implies that if wage rates do not alter in the short run, there will be no unemployment. In the longer term, however, the equilibrium is at e and the capital stock must fall implying as before that real wages must fall if full employment is to be maintained.

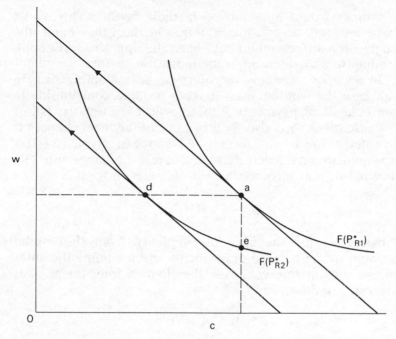

Figure 2.13   *Energy and the factor price frontier*

Energy Windfalls

When the prices of raw materials and oil change, all countries are affected. This chapter's concern with these issues has reflected the essentially international character of the present study. Parochial problems pertaining to specific economies have been expressly avoided in the search for a global analysis of the slowdown in the West. However, we will now depart temporarily from this by considering the structural effects of energy windfalls such as have befallen countries like Norway and the UK. As we shall see, these windfalls tend to generate deindustrialization in the sense described earlier in this chapter. But this in no sense implies that, for example, North Sea oil is a curse and that the UK would have been better off without the oil discoveries.

In a closed economy an oil windfall (indeed any windfall) might have affected the structure of relative prices. In so far as, say, non-industrial output comprises superior goods their relative price would have risen and the allocation of resources would have moved in their favour. This would have induced de-industrialisation. On the other hand, the engle curve effects might have been the opposite way about, leading to an expansion in the industrial sector.

In an open economy the outcome is less ambiguous. In this case the windfall must make a positive contribution to the balance of payments, either because oil imports fall or because oil exports rise. This balance of payments benefit is denoted below by X. The non-oil balance of payments (B) is assumed to vary inversely with the real exchange rate (R) and permanent income which in turn depends on X:

$$B = -\alpha_1 R - \alpha_2 X$$

Abstracting for the sake of simplicity from the capital account of the balance of payments and assuming the authorities do not intervene, i.e. the float is free, the market clearing condition is:

$$B + X = 0$$

which implies:

$$R = \frac{1 - \alpha_2}{\alpha_1} X$$

Assuming $\alpha_2 < 1$, on the grounds that at the margin permanent income is not entirely spent on traded goods, the real exchange rate varies directly with the oil windfall. Hence the windfall generates two benefits:

● The direct benefit of the windfall itself.
● The indirect terms of trade benefit induced by the increase in the real exchange rate.

The latter goes to zero either as $\alpha_2 = 1$, i.e. as all the direct benefit is spent on traded goods, or as $\alpha_1 = \infty$, i.e. as domestic and overseas traded goods are perfect substitutes. For the UK Beenstock, Budd and Warburton (1981) estimate that by 1980 North Sea oil had raised the real exchange rate by about 14 per cent since 1975. Forsyth and Kay (1980) suggest a 12 per cent appreciation. The greater the real exchange rate effect, the greater is the terms of trade benefit. Since the deterioration in the non-oil balance (B) must always equal $(1 - \alpha_2)\Delta X$ it is in the national interest that the real exchange rate effect should be as large as possible. This contrasts with the often-voiced argument that this effect is disadvantageous.

If $\alpha_2 < 1$ the oil balance crowds out the non-oil balance. Domestic consumption of tradeables rises by $\alpha_2\Delta X$ so that consumption of non-tradeables must rise by $(1 - \alpha_2)\Delta X$. Where do these non-tradeables come from? By definition they cannot be imported, therefore they must be provided by de-industrialisation, as resources shift from the production of tradeables to the production of non-tradeables. Thus de-industrialisation is an inevitable and desirable consequence of an oil windfall, assuming the marginal propensity to consume tradeables (α_2) is less than unity. Without it we could not enjoy the benefits of North Sea oil to the full extent.

A similar analysis applies when the real price of oil rises since this brings about an increase in X. In this case de-industrialisation occurs for two reasons:

- Production function effects along the lines discussed in relation to Figure 2.6
- Balance of payments effects along the lines discussed in the present section.

The balance of payments effect applies to countries such as Japan which have no energy (or raw materials) sectors but with reversed sign. It also applies to net oil importers such as West Germany. In this case an increase in oil prices must reduce X, because oil import bills rise. Therefore the balance of payments effect increases the relative size of the industrial or traded goods sector, since B must rise to compensate for the deterioration in X. On the other hand, the production function effects will still be de-industrialising in nature. This ambiguous story is explored in Figure 2.14, where the vertical axis measures the relative price of tradeables while the horizontal axis measures total output. D' represents the domestic demand for tradeables and varies

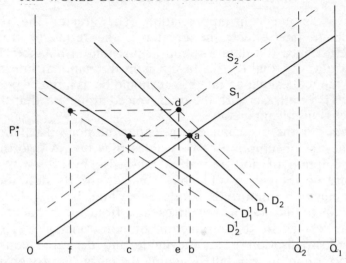

Figure 2.14 *Energy, the balance of payments and de-industrialisation*

inversely with their relative price. D represents the total
demand for tradeables, i.e. including the overseas demand
which varies inversely with the real exchange rate (R).
Therefore D − D' is the net foreign demand. S denotes the
supply schedule for tradeables. Since total output is given,
the higher P_1^* is, the higher the production of tradeables and
the lower the production of non-tradeables.

The initial equilibrium is at a where the demand and supply of tradeables are equal. Output of tradeables is Ob of
which Oc are consumed by residents and cb are exported to
pay for energy imports of X_1. The production of non-
tradeables is therefore equal to bQ_1.

We now assume that the price of energy rises so that
aggregate supply falls by Q_2Q_1. However the traded goods
sector is disproportionately affected so that the upward shift
in S to S_2 is greater than Q_2Q_1. On the other hand energy
import bills rise to X_2 (assuming plausible energy demand
elasticities), so that the non-oil trade balance has to improve.
In Figure 2.14 this improvement is represented by the difference between fe and cb where fe > cb. The contraction in
D' is proportionate to the fall in aggregate supply, hence D_2
must pass through d. Net foreign demand has risen reflecting

the fall in the real exchange rate, and the new equilibrium is at d where D_2 and S_2 intersect.

Output of tradeables is Oe and output of non-tradeables is eQ_2. What has happened to the share of tradeables in total output? The production function effect has reduced it but the balance of payments effect has increased it. De-industrialisation takes place as

$$\frac{Oe}{OQ_2} < \frac{Ob}{OQ_1}$$

It is clear from Figure 2.14 that if the balance of payments effects were sufficiently large D_2 might intersect S_2 to the north-east of a. In this case not only is the de-industrialisation condition violated but the production of tradeables rises absolutely.

The Bank of England (1982) and Byatt *et al.* (1982) assume that an increase in the price of oil must raise the share of tradeables and therefore manufacturing output in the economies of oil importing countries such as West Germany and Japan. Their argument is that to pay for their higher oil import bills these countries must devote a larger proportion of output to traded goods and this will raise the share of manufacturing in total output. They seem to rule out the possibility that these bills may be paid by reducing domestic absorption, and it is simple to demonstrate that their assumptions are incorrect.

We assume that in the oil manufacturing country the manufacturing sector is energy intensive so that, *ceteris paribus*, when the price of energy (P_e) rises the relative supply of manufacturing output (S) declines. We also assume that the relative allocation of resources to the manufacturing sector varies directly with the relative price of manufactures (P). Hence the relative supply schedule may be written in linear terms as:

$$S = -\alpha_1 P_e + \alpha_2 P$$

The relative demand (D) for manufactures will vary directly with P_e because higher oil import bills must be paid for out of manufactures. Domestic disposable income will fall for two reasons. First, the terms of trade loss will adversely affect disposable income. Secondly, the higher price of energy inputs will reduce aggregate supply. If manufactures are inferior goods the resulting fall in domestic disposable income will raise the relative demand for manufactures. Therefore, the sign of β_1 in the equation below is ambiguous. This equation also assumes that relative demand varies inversely with relative prices. Hence:

$$D = \beta_1 P_e - \beta_2 P \qquad \beta_1 \lessgtr 0$$

Equating relative supply and demand implies that the equilibrium relative price is:

$$P^* = \frac{\beta_1 + \alpha_1}{\alpha_2 + \beta_2} P_e$$

This in turn implies that the relationship between relative output and the price of oil is:

$$S = \frac{\beta_1(\alpha_2 - \alpha_1)}{\alpha_2 + \beta_2} P_e$$

This implies that the relative size of the manufacturing sector for an oil importing country does not have an unambiguous relationship with the price of oil. If β_1 is positive and $\alpha_2 > \alpha_1$, the effect will be positive as the Bank of England and Byatt *et al.* assume.

For oil exporters the higher oil price unambiguously reduces the relative size of the manufacturing sector, because the aggregate supply and terms of trade effects work in the same direction. Table 2.5 summarises the taxonomy of possibilities. The production function effect refers to the response of producers who transfer resources away from the manufacturing sector under the assumption that it is relatively energy intensive. In the above model this effect is denoted by the coefficient α_1. The income effect refers to the effect of oil prices on disposable income and the pattern of domestic demand. The terms of trade effect refers to the effect of oil prices on the allocation of resources into the balance of payments. Section A is concerned with the effect of an oil price rise and distinguishes whether countries are

Table 2.5   *Oil and de-industrialisation*

	Production function	Income	Terms of trade	Net
A Oil price rise				
1 Oil exporters	−	?	−	−
2 Oil importers	−	?	+	?
B Oil discovery	−			−

net importers or exporters of oil or energy. Case A2 is the one discussed above. The net effect is ambiguous because the terms of trade and production function effects have opposite signs while the income effect is indeterminate since it depends on the engle curves with respect to domestic disposable income.

The latter ambiguity also applies to case A1. Higher oil prices raise net exporters' disposable incomes and much will depend on how this additional income is spent on manufactures and non-manufactures. The terms of trade effect is negative because exporters need to sell less non-oil tradeables abroad to purchase a given volume of imports. The net effect on the share of manufacturing output is therefore likely to be negative although the ambiguity of the income effect means that in principle the net effect is ambiguous too. Finally Section B reminds us that oil discoveries are de-industrialising as already argued, regardless of net oil trade status.

The case of the UK is interesting because at various times all aspects of this taxonomy have applied. In 1973–4 the UK was an oil importer when OPEC raised oil prices and oil production was zero. Therefore case A2 applied. During the second half of the 1970s North Sea oil began to flow, therefore case B applied. By 1981 the UK had become a net oil exporter in which case A1 applies not only with regard to future oil price changes but also retroactively with respect to oil price changes in the 1970s. Therefore at present cases A1 and B apply to the UK, which means that there have been two sources of de-industrialisation.

3

Transition Theory

I Introduction

Critique of Global Theories

In this chapter we continue with our search for a global theory of economic decline in the West. This does not necessarily imply that the hypotheses considered in Chapter 2 are inadequate; no doubt they contain elements of truth. Therefore what will be said in this chapter should be viewed as complementary to what has already been said in Chapter 2. Nevertheless, there are two fairly obvious problems with these theories.

First, Cornwall's theory of technology diffusion does not imply a relatively abrupt slowdown. Instead a gradual levelling-off in economic growth rates is implied, as laggard countries close the technology gap. However, as noted in Chapter 1, what in fact happened was a relatively abrupt slowdown. But to be fair to him, Cornwall was not explicitly concerned with explaining the abrupt nature of the slowdown.

Second, the obvious appeal of the Bruno–Sachs thesis is that the revolution in commodity prices coincided with the slowdown. This begs the question why real commodity prices changed in the first place. Bruno and Sachs take the shift in these prices as a datum and offer no explanations. In this context it should be noted that Bruno and Sachs reverse the more conventional causal relationships between the level of world economic activity and commodity prices. The conventional view is that commodity prices are driven by the level of world economic activity. This thesis is incorporated in the econometric models referenced in Chapter 1, as well as in numerous other studies, such as Panic and Enoch (1981). In contrast Bruno and Sachs maintain that the level of world economic activity is driven by commodity prices.

The truth most probably lies between these positions, so that commodity prices and world output are jointly determined. In so far as this is the case the econometric work of Bruno and Sachs will be biased, since they ignore reverse causality. By the same token the conventional wisdom will be biased also.

Outline of the Thesis

The Transition Theory developed in this chapter is concerned with the evolving relationships between the developed and developing countries of the world. The theory has two particular advantages. First, it explains the abrupt nature of the slowdown. Secondly, it explains the revolution in raw materials prices. The word 'transition' itself distinguishes the theory, because it implies that the world economy is moving from one equilibrium to another over time, according to an economic realignment between developed and developing countries.

The basic insight of the theory is that developing countries have been 'taking off' and in the process have threatened the developed countries. This threat has largely been felt in the manufacturing sector through the media of international trade and investment. Specifically, developing countries have been out-performing industrialised countries in international trade. They have been exporting to OECD countries at the expense of indigenous OECD suppliers and they have been import substituting. Indeed Lewis (1978a) argues that they first replaced OECD suppliers in their own (LDC) markets. Once they had pushed this process to its limits they moved on to compete with OECD producers on their home ground. On the other hand, in his Nobel Lecture Lewis (1980) reiterates the orthodox view that slower economic growth in the North will reduce the demand for exports from the South which will weaken the LDC balance of payments. This in turn will reduce the South's capacity to import from the North, which will reduce LDC economic growth.

Through this conventional transmission mechanism the slow-down in the North induces a slowdown in the developing countries. Indeed, Lewis explores the assumption that the heyday of LDC growth is over because the heyday of DC growth is over.

In addition, capital in developing countries has been out-competing capital in OECD countries in the sense that the rate of return on LDC capital has risen relative to the rate of return on capital in OECD countries. This has brought about a transfer of capital from the OECD to the LDC bloc, and this transfer of capital has strengthened growth in the developing countries and undermined it in the industrialized countries.

Therefore in terms both of international trade and of international investment the developing countries have been 'crowding out' the developed countries, especially since the mid-1960s when many developing countries adopted an outward-looking development strategy. This shift in the bal-ance of economic power has not only affected world relative prices, it has also required the OECD countries to re-structure their economies. The recession in the West has been brought about by this restructuring; the economic up-heavals that have taken place since about 1970 have been a consequence of a major realignment in the balance of world industrial power. In theory, the restructuring could have gone smoothly. In the West, resources could have moved out of the threatened steel and textile industries into other, new activities in which growth was taking place. In practice, how-ever, resources have not been able to redeploy themselves so easily and industries have been dying faster than new ones have been born.

In time the full transition will be achieved. However, while it is in progress the economies of the West undergo what amounts to a sustained recession. It is certainly no coincidence that the world recession missed the developing countries during the 1970s despite all the predictions that recession in the West would spread to developing countries. On the contrary, the recession in the West has been partly brought about by the impressive growth performance of the developing countries. This is the implication of the Transition Theory.The Transition Theory has several logical steps:

(1) From the mid-1960s economic growth in the developing countries increased (see Table 1.4). This was particularly pronounced in the manufacturing sector.

(2) The disproportionate increase in the supply of manufactured products that resulted from LDC industrialisation caused the relative price of manufactures on world markets to decline. The commodity price explosion of the 1970s was as much a fall in the price of manufactures relative to commodities as a rise in the price of commodities relative to manufactures.

(3) This relative price shift reduced economic incentives in the West with respect to the production of manufactures, triggering de-industrialisation across the OECD as a whole. This was accompanied by increased competition in manufactures on the part of developing countries in OECD markets.

(4) LDC industrialisation raised the return on capital relative to the rate of return on capital in OECD countries. This induced the export of capital from the OECD bloc to the LDCs, lowering OECD investment and raising LDC investment. Consequently productivity growth in developed countries was reduced.

(5) As OECD economies adjust to the change in relative prices and the lower capital stock, structural unemployment grows. It takes time before redundant steelworkers can move into other occupations. In certain sectors labour is scarce while in the manufacturing sector there is an excess supply of labour. Below we call this 'mismatch' unemployment. It is not a paradox but an implication of the Transition Theory.

(6) Once the transition is complete, mismatch unemployment disappears but the reallocation of the world capital stock in favour of the LDCs and the decline in OECD terms of trade implies that real incomes in the OECD bloc will be lower than if the LDCs had not industrialised. The distribution of world output and income has moved in favour of the developing countries.

The new steady-state represented by Stage 6 may not be very different, as far as OECD real income is concerned, from what it originally was. The real problems arise with the transition during Stage 5, rather than after the transition is complete. The experience of the 1970s suggests that the upheavals during the transition may be large; however, by definition, they must be temporary. This suggests that the recession in the West will eventually come to an end unless there are further expansions of growth in the Third World. But even if there are none, it is suggested in Chapter 6 that the transition phase may be with us until the end of the century.

The Conventional Wisdom

'Among the greatest challenges to international economic policy for the rest of this century is the preparation for a new deployment of industrial capacity in the world economy – a shift of historic dimensions' (The Brandt Report, p. 177, in reference to the industrialisation of the developing countries).

From this quotation it might be concluded that the Transition Theory has formed part of the conventional wisdom and that it is generally recognised that the slowdown in the West is bound up with the economic progress of the developing countries. The opposite is the case; it has generally been concluded that so far the LDCs have not been an economic threat to the industrialised countries. Indeed p. 176 of the Brandt Report agrees with this conclusion, despite what it goes on to say on p. 177.

There have been several studies of the effect of OECD–LDC trade on OECD employment. They typically conclude that either the effect is negative but very small, e.g. Foreign and Commonwealth Office (1979), or that it is small and positive, e.g. OECD (1979). The calculations refer to net employment effects. However, the reports admit that in certain sectors, such as textiles, the gross employment effects may be substantial. Since these and similar reports provide the basis for the present conventional wisdom their methodologies will be examined in some detail.

The basic methodology was originally developed by Cable (1978). Since output (Q) is defined as

$$Q = H + X - M$$

where

$$H = \text{home demand}$$
$$X = \text{exports}$$
$$M = \text{imports}$$

and productivity is defined as

$$P = Q/L$$

where

$$L = \text{employment}$$

it follows that the change in employment may be defined as

$$\Delta L_t = (\Delta H_t + \Delta X_t - \Delta M_t - L_t \Delta P_t)/P_{t-1}$$

This equation contains no economic theory; it is a definition and must always be true. It states that the change in employment depends negatively on productivity growth for given levels of employment and positively on the change in output for given levels of productivity. The equation may be disaggregated by SITC (Standard International Trade Classification) category and by trading partner. Hence it is possible to calculate the employment effects of, say, imports of textiles from Hong Kong as well as the employment effects of exports of machinery to Korea. This is the methodology used in the official reports cited above. It has some fairly obvious shortcomings:

- It assumes that home demand, exports, imports and productivity are independent of one another when in fact there is a complex relationship between them.
- It ignores the effects of LDC competition in third markets, e.g. loss of export markets to Korea.
- It implies that improvements in productivity must cause unemployment, i.e. it assumes labour markets do not exist.
- It ignores the indirect effects of relative price effects and

international investment effects in stages 3 and 4 of the Transition Theory.
● To calculate the net employment effect of LDC exports it is necessary to determine what LDC imports would have been in the absence of these exports. The methodology makes no allowance for this.
● In short, the methodology provides no basis for the conventional view about the effects of LDC growth on OECD economies.

Within the academic community there has been little analysis of the effects of LDC industrialisation on the economic prospects of the developed countries. Indeed all the studies mentioned so far have been produced by government or quasi-governmental institutions in one form or another. However, Kreuger (1980) takes the view that the LDC manufacturing sector is too small to affect OECD comparative advantage in manufactures and therefore she is in broad support of the conventional wisdom. In contrast Fröbel *et al*. (1980) argue that the integration of the LDCs in the world manufacturing economy has created a new international division of labour which has undermined the economic position of workers in the developed countries and not improved the prospect of workers in the developing countries. They arrive at these conclusions on the basis of case studies of West German firms that have established foreign subsidiaries in Asia, Africa and South America. These studies show that over the period 1960–76 the subsidiaries expanded employment at a faster rate than their parent counterparts and that in many instances parent company employment fell by as much as 25 per cent. They thus paint a picture in which trade and capital movements are closely related; West German firms have been relocating in the Third World and have been supplying West German and third country markets from abroad instead of from West Germany. It is, however, difficult to extrapolate from this evidence and deduce that the LDC threat to the West German economy is large. Nor do the authors establish that 'trickle down' has failed to work in those LDCs where manufacturing output has increased. Instead they seem to be more concerned with establishing the Marxist thesis that capital conspires against labour by exploiting cheap labour in the Third World and by reducing the bargaining power of workers in the industrialised countries in the process.

Another argument for the conventional view is that the LDCs' share in the consumption of manufactures in the industrialised countries is very low, as may be seen in Table 3.1. By 1978 the LDC share was less than 3 per cent although this proportion had risen substantially since 1970. How, it is argued, can the LDCs seriously disrupt the economies of the industrialised countries when their share of consumption of manufactures is so low? The fallacy in this argument is similar to the fallacy with the employment formula; it ignores indirect effects and third country effects. It makes more sense to look at the LDCs' share of world manufacturing output and world trade as shown in Table 3.2. This table suggests that the LDCs are large enough to play a significant role in the world market for manufactures. Their share of output has risen significantly since the mid-1960s while their trade share has approximately doubled over the same period.

The earlier point that the employment formula fails to take account of intra-LDC trade effects is underlined by

Table 3.1 *LDC share of consumption of manufactures in some industrialised countries 1970–8 (%)*

	1970	1978
Australia	2.1	4.8
Canada	1.2	1.9
Belgium	5.6	4.2
France	2.1	2.6
West Germany	2.3	4.1
Italy	2.1	3.9
Netherlands	4.9	7.4
United Kingdom	3.3	4.8
Japan	1.3	1.5
Sweden	2.8	3.1
United States	1.2	2.9
AVERAGE	1.7	2.9

Source: World Bank (1981) Table 3.3

Table 3.2   *LDC share of world manufac-*
turing output and trade 1950–80 (% in
1975 dollars)

	Output	Trade
1950	8.4	
1960	10.3	4.4
1965	10.4	5.1
1970	11.75	5.6
1975	14.9	6.9
1980	15.5	9.8

Source: *Yearbook of International Trade Statistics*
(New York: UN) various issues
Note: excludes centrally planned economies

Table 3.3, which shows how intra-LDC trade in manufactures has grown much faster than LDC trade with developed countries. The table shows that after 1968 export growth increased and that this growth was to some extent directed at developed countries. However, the remarkable feature of Table 3.3 is the large increase in the growth of intra-LDC trade, suggesting that not only were LDCs competing directly in OECD domestic markets but that they were also making inroads into OECD external markets.

The conventional wisdom that LDC influence on the economic fortunes of developed countries has been insignificant may therefore be repudiated. In the rest of this chapter we argue that most probably the opposite is true. Moreover, the LDC–DC relationship is more complex than was previously supposed. In Section II the Transition Theory which explores this relationship is described in greater detail. Chapter 4 reviews the data which on the whole suggests that

Table 3.3   *Growth of LDC manufactured exports by destination*
1960–78 (% p.a. at 1970 prices)

	To developed countries	To LDCs	Total
1960–8	9.7	9	9.2
1968–78	11.2	14.7	12.3

Source: *Monthly Bulletin of Statistics* (New York: UN, July 1980) Special Table F

the Transition Theory is valid. Indeed the political manifestation of this process is the rise of 'new protectionism', which
has penalized certain industrial economies such as Japan but
has also involved numerous developing countries. Voluntary
export restraints have been negotiated by industrial countries (the US and the EEC in particular) with Korea, Argentina, Indonesia, Mexico and a host of other LDCs. The
renegotiation of the Multi-fibre Agreement has become a
vehicle for restricting trade in textiles to the particular disadvantage of developing countries. Helleiner (1979) has
argued that the new protectionism is mainly directed at
activities which are intensive in unskilled labour, i.e. in precisely those activities where the LDCs have a competitive
advantage.

This political manifestation indicates that the conventional wisdom is invalid; there is no smoke without fire. The
Transition Theory attempts to clarify some of the economic
processes involved in this conflagration.

II   Theoretical Analysis

Stage 1: LDC Growth

The six stages of the Transition Theory summarised on
p. 61 are not necessarily chronological. Their main purpose
is functional and they provide a framework for organising
the discussion. Certain stages will be contemporaneous,
others will overlap and some may be sequential. For example, the process of LDC industrialisation which is the
starting point of the Transition Theory is not independent
of Stage 4, which concerns capital exports to LDCs.

Figure 3.1 characterises the secular economic expansion
that took place in the LDCs around the mid-1960s. To sim-
plify matters we assume a two-sector model in which LDCs
produce non-manufactures and manufactures which are
measured along the vertical and horizontal axes respectively.
Initially the production possibility frontier is assumed to be
$T_1T_1^1$ which measures the combinations of the two outputs
which the LDCs can produce given the size of their capital
stock and labour force and given the state of technology,

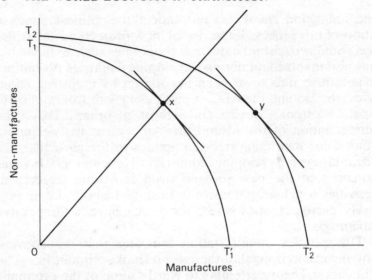

Figure 3.1 *LDC industrialisation*

infrastructure etc. This production possibility frontier is a snap-shot of what is in effect a dynamic phenomenon since technology, capital etc. change over time. Nevertheless the static representation is adequate for present purposes and has the merits of simplicity. Given the relative price of manufactures, the optimal production mix will be determined at x and the slope of O_x reflects the share of non-manufactures in total output.

LDC industrialisation is characterized by an autonomous expansion in the production possibility frontier from $T_1T_1^1$ to $T_2T_2^1$. LDCs can now produce more of both outputs, but this transformation has favoured the manufacturing sector. This is the static analogue to the expansion in GDP growth after the mid-1960s (see Table 1.4) and the rise in the share of manufacturing in total LDC output. The shift in the production possibility frontier is autonomous, in the sense that more can be produced at existing factor allocations. Hence if we denote the aggregate production function as

$$Q = \lambda_1 F(\lambda_2 K, \lambda_3 L)$$

Q may rise because either λ_1, λ_2 or λ_3 rise at given levels of K (capital stock) and L (employment). If λ_1 rises this will be equivalent to Hicks' neutral technical progress. However, the shifts in λ do not reflect technical progress. Instead this autonomous development reflects the fact that the LDCs have, after decades of inertia, at last put their act together and are rumbling down the road of economic development which Western economies took over the previous two centuries. Precisely what makes for industrial revolution has eluded economic historians for generations. But our starting point is that the pre-conditions have been fulfilled, the spark has been lit and that largely for these autonomous reasons industrialisation is afoot in the LDCs.

We recognise, as Table 3.4 indicates, that LDC growth performance has not been uniformly good. During the 1970s manufacturing growth failed to sustain itself in the low income countries, although GDP growth held up well. These figures also conceal large differences even within the bloc of middle income countries. Compare, for example, the poor performance of Zambia (0.8) and Senegal (-0.2) with the outstanding performance of Korea (7.1), Hong Kong (7.0) and Brazil (4.8). While recognising these differences, in what follows we abstract from them; not because they are unimportant but because they do not affect the broad thrust of the argument.

While LDC industrialisation is treated as an autonomous phenomenon it is possible to say something more about why this transformation took place. A gathering consensus, as exemplified in various of the World Bank's *World Development Reports*, is that LDC industrial progress since the mid-1960s reflects the adoption of an outward-looking

Table 3.4 *Distribution of LDC growth rates 1960–79 (% p.a.)*

	GDP	Industrial production	Manufacturing
Low-income countries			
1960–70	4.5	6.6	6.5
1970–79	4.7	4.2	3.7
Middle-income countries			
1960–70	6.1	7.4	7.0
1970–79	5.5	6.5	6.6

Source: World Bank (1981) Table 2

development strategy instead of the inward-looking strategy that had been in vogue since the end of the Second World War. By 'inward-looking' is meant a strategy based on import substitution, by 'outward-looking' a strategy based on export promotion. In the former case LDCs would set up tariff barriers to keep out foreign imports (including imports from other LDCs) in an attempt to stimulate domestic production. The main economic argument was the need for 'infant industry' protection to help fledgling industries develop. In practice, infancy was rarely followed by adulthood and it was impossible to remove the protective tariffs. Instead economic inefficiency became institutionalised. A side effect of this policy was the emergence of discrepancies between effective and nominal rates of protection as evidenced by the research of Balassa *et al.* (1971). Nominal tariffs designed to protect industry X act as taxes on other activities for which X is an intermediate input. The confusion between nominal and effective rates of protection made an import substitution policy extremely hazardous.

Inward-looking policies regard the home market as the principal outlet for protectionism. This is fine so long as the home market is large and expanding. These conditions did not apply in LDCs. Lewis (1978a) points out that this inward-looking preoccupation that was prevalent after the Second World War reflected interwar experience. The collapse of world markets, especially during the 1930s, implied that the home market was the principal source of trading stability. In addition, colonial administrations bequeathed an inward-looking economic philosophy to the newly independent nations such as India. Therefore inward-looking development policies had political as well as economic justifications at the time.

Inward-looking strategy began to supplant them from the mid-1960s. This strategy essentially assumed two forms: neutral and aggressive. The neutral version revised the restrictive policies of the inward-looking strategy. Tariffs were lowered and subsidies to import substitution were either lowered or removed. The world market was placed on an equal footing with the home market. In the aggressive version the world market was placed at a premium and export bounties were offered by governments to increase manufacturing for exports. The advantages of this outward orientation lie in the exploitation of a large and dynamic world market, the removal of distortions to production and the opening up of the developing economies to foreign investment and technology. The contributions of the outward orientation to economic development have been reviewed in the 1979 *World Development Report* of the World Bank and by Balassa (1981). Although the outward orientation is by no means universally adopted, it is approved by most development agencies and the success stories of Korea, Brazil, Singapore, etc, are quoted in its support.

It is widely argued that the achievement of LDC industrialisation reflects the adoption of a more outward orientation from the mid-1960s. This may or may not be so, although the arguments seem plausible enough. An alternative and perhaps complementary viewpoint is that the ingredients of industrialisation are as much social as economic. Rapid urbanisation and the advancement of literacy and numeracy (see Table 1.6) have paved the way for industrialisation. There is an almost Gestalt-like discontinuity as societies begin to industrialise. The special X factor that makes the spark seems to be more deeply rooted in social attitudes than in inward-versus-outward orientations, no matter how important this issue may be.

Industrialisation is therefore taken here to be a matter of fact. In Figure 3.1, if relative prices remain unchanged the economy will settle down at y, along the new production possibility frontier. At y the share of manufacturing in GDP has risen and the output of non-manufactures has increased. If, however, relative prices move in favour of non-manufactures the optimal production point will be to the left of y along $T_2T_2^1$. We shall return to this possibility at a later stage.

Stage 2: World Prices

For expositional simplicity we assume that all output is traded. In a more general analysis we might consider a three-sector model which differentiates between primary, secondary and tertiary output respectively. In an appendix to this chapter a three-sector model is considered. However,

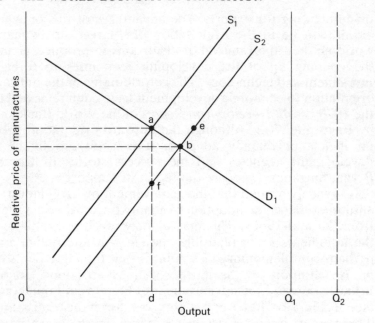

Figure 3.2 *The market for world output*

as this section proceeds it will be pointed out how the tertiary sector might be affected.

Let us assume for the sake of argument that y on Figure 3.1 lies horizontally to the right of x, i.e. at unchanged relative prices the output of manufactures rises but primary production is not affected. What effect will this disturbance have on world markets? Figure 3.2 is designed to answer this question. D_1 denotes the demand schedule for manufactures relative to non manufactures. As the relative price of manufactures falls, the relative demand for manufactures rises. The absolute demand for manufactures is equal to the horizontal distance between D_1 and the relative price axis. The absolute demand for non-manufactures is equal to the horizontal distance between D_1 and the perpendicular to Q_1. OQ_1 is the initial supply of output (equal to income) as a whole. Thus if the relative price of manufactures falls from a to b the demand for manufactures rises from Od to Oc and the demand for non-manufactures falls from dQ_1 to cQ_1. S_1 represents the initial relative supply curve for manufactures and is analogous to the demand curve. Thus as the relative price of manufactures rises the relative supply of manufactures rises. The absolute supply of manufactures is read horizontally from the left and the absolute supply of non-manufactures is measured horizontally from the right.

Initially, world output is OQ_1, the demand curve is D_1 and the supply curve is S_1. The market for world output is therefore in equilibrium at a; the supply of manufactures equals the demand for manufactures and supply equals demand in the market for non-manufactures. The autonomous increase in LDC output is represented by an increase in world output from OQ_1 to OQ_2. Since by assumption this expansion is entirely concentrated in the manufacturing sector the relative supply curve for manufactures must move horizontally to the right by Q_1Q_2, i.e. from S_1 to S_2. The demand curve is likely to move too. However, in the interest of preserving the simplicity of the figure we assume that all the extra LDC income is spent on non-manufactures. Therefore the demand curve on Figure 3.2 does not move.

The new equilibrium is at b. The supply and demand for manufactures is Oc and for non-manufactures it is cQ_2. The relative price of manufactures has declined from da to cb. Alternatively, the relative price of primary products in terms of manufactures has risen.

If

$$\frac{dc}{Q_1Q_2} > \frac{Od}{OQ_1}$$

the share of manufacturing in world output will rise. Clearly what happens to this ratio is ambiguous, since it mostly depends on the shape of the engle curves in the LDCs. As we have noted, if more of the income increase is spent on manufactures the equilibrium is at b. If, instead, all of it is spent on manufactures, the equilibrium will be at e and the relative price of manufactures will be unchanged. Under normal circumstances the new equilibrium would be between b and e. A second source of ambiguity is the slope of the demand curve. The more elastic the demand curve the closer b will be to e in which case the inequality condition is more likely to be fulfilled. If, however, the demand curve is completely inelastic, D_1 will intersect S_2 at f, in which case the inequality condition cannot be met. Also the relative price increase of primary products will be more pronounced. Yet a third source of ambiguity concerns our initial assumption that expansion of output is exclusively in the manufacturing sector. In so far as non-manufacturing output also rises, the fall in the relative price of manufactures will be smaller and the inequality condition will stand a smaller chance of being met.

Stage 3: De-industrialisation in the West

Under the plausible assumption that relative prices have moved against manufactures, what are the economic consequences for the developed countries? To answer this question Figure 3.3 has been developed; it is based on the familiar Edgeworth box diagram. The horizontal axis measures the capital stock; the vertical axis measures employment. From the origin O is measured the output of non-manufactures; from the origin O^1 is measured the output of manufactures. The capital stock is initially assumed to be OK_1 and the

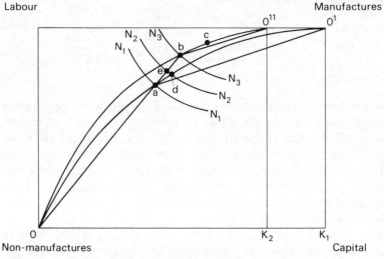

Figure 3.3   *De-industrialisation in developed economies*

labour supply is fixed at its full employment level. O^1aO represents the efficiency locus of the isoquant tangents and corresponds with a production possibility frontier such as is shown on Figure 3.1. As we move north-east along this locus, production of non-manufactures rises while production of manufactures falls. The convexity of this locus with respect to the labour axis implies that non-manufactures are labour intensive and that manufactures are capital intensive. This assumption reflects the previous discussion in Chapter 2.

Given the initial world relative price of manufactures producers will maximise profits by choosing a point such as a on the efficiency locus. N_1N_1 is the isoquant for non-manufactures that passes through a and the slope of the tangent at a reflects the wage relative to the returns to capital. When the relative price of manufactures declines producers in developed countries will respond by producing less manufactures and more non-manufactures. In terms of Figure 3.3 we explore this issue under two assumptions. First, we assume that the capital is fixed at OK_1. Secondly, we assume that the capital stock falls from OK_1 to OK_2. This has several justifications. First, as argued in Chapter 2, a more complex model implies that the capital stock tends to fall when the price of raw materials rises. However, in the present model raw materials are not separately identified. Secondly, as argued under Stage 4 of the theory, capital is likely to be exported from the developed to the developing countries.

If the capital stock remains fixed, the increased production of non-manufactures is represented by a north-easterly movement along the efficiency locus from a to d. The Stolper–Samuelson (1941) theorem implies that at d the share of wages in GDP will have risen, because the marginal product of labour (and therefore real wage rates) has risen relative to the marginal product of capital. This must be so, because at e along isoquant N_2N_2 the marginal rate of substitution between capital and labour is the same as at a (because a and e lie on the same ray from the origin O). At d the marginal rate of substitution is lower than at e, so it must be lower than at a. This suggests that as the relative price of manufactures falls there will be de-industrialisation in developed countries coupled with a rise in the wage share.

If the capital stock falls by K_1K_2 the efficiency locus will become $O^{11}cbO$. According to the Rybczynski (1955) theorem the contraction in the capital stock will generate b as the optimal production point along the new efficiency locus, assuming the original set of relative prices still applies. The reason for this is that the marginal rate of substitution at b is the same as at a and $O^{11}b$ is parallel to O^1a, i.e. capital–labour ratios are unchanged. At b total output is lower, the output of non-manufactures has risen and the output of manufactures is lower. Because the capital stock is lower the wage share rises. However, b cannot be an optimal production mix because the relative price of manufactures has fallen. As in the previous case this implies a north-easterly movement along the efficiency locus to a point such as c. Hence, de-industrialisation becomes more pronounced and the wage share further increased.

In the summary the Stage 3 effects are these:

- The share of manufactures in output declines in developed countries.
- The wage share rises (the profit share falls).

If we allow for the existence of a tertiary sector it seems likely that the relative price shift will move resources out of manufactures into tertiary activities as well as primary production. Many industrialised countries do not possess significant primary sectors; instead they are required to import primary production. In this case the model proposed in Chapter 2 applies. Nevertheless, the tertiary sector is likely to expand and the profit share decline.

Let us, however, continue with the assumption that all non-manufactures are traded and let us further assume that LDCs are net exporters of non-manufactures and DCs are net exporters of manufactures. Hence LDCs are net importers of manufactures and DCs are net importers of non-manufactures. On Figure 3.4 we re-draw Figure 3.1 in the top segment and in the lower segment we draw the production frontier for the developed countries that corresponds with the efficiency locus O^1daO in Figure 3.3. At the initial set of relative prices (P_1) the LDC production point is x and the consumption point is assumed to be m.

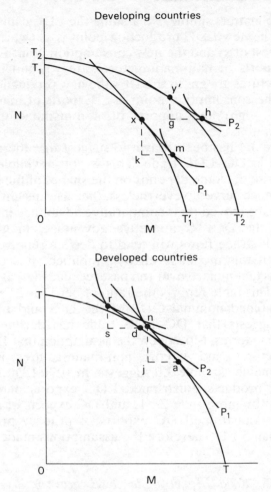

Figure 3.4 *International trade between developing and developed countries*

Therefore LDCs export xk of non-manufactures and import km of manufactures. In the DCs the production point is represented by a and the consumption point by n, in which case the DCs export ja (= km) of manufactures and import jn (= xk) of non-manufactures.

At the new set of relative prices (P$_2$), the price of manufactures has fallen relative to the price of non-manufactures and the LDC production possibility frontier has expanded.

To keep matters simple, we assume the LDC capital stock is fixed. The new LDC production point is y^1 (which must be north-west of x) and the new consumption point is h. Therefore exports of non-manufactures are y^1g and imports of manufactures are gh. In the DCs the new production point is d and the consumption point is r. Exports of manufactures are sd (= gh) and imports of non-manufactures are rs (= y^1g).

Figure 3.4 has been drawn to suggest that there is a contraction in DC–LDC trade. This is not inevitable, because the precise outcome depends on the shapes of the respective indifference curves. Nevertheless, the basic insight is that the LDCs have moved their comparative advantage in the direction of the DCs' comparative advantage, in which case LDC–DC trade flows will tend to decline relative to GDP. Although this model is highly simplified, it accords with what has taken place over the past two decades, as Table 3.5 shows. This table reports the ratio of net DC–LDC trade to the combined nominal GDP of the DCs and LDCs. The table suggests that DC–LDC trade has declined in proportionate terms. Moreover, the assumption that DCs export manufactures and import non-manufactures is not so unreasonable as Table 3.6 suggests. In 1970 LDC exports of primary products outstripped LDC exports of secondary products by more than 2 : 1, and DC exports of secondary products outstripped DC exports of primary products by more than 5 : 1. Therefore the assumptions made in Figure

Table 3.5   *Ratio of net trade flows between developed and developing countries to nominal world GDP 1960–78*

	1 *Exports of LDCs to DCs + exports of DCs to LDCs ($ bn)*	2 *GDP of DCs and LDCs ($ bn)*	*Ratio of 1 to 2 (%)*
1960	41.66	1137	3.66
1970	81.99	2477	3.31
1978	225.0[a]	7120	3.16

Source: Yearbook of International Trade Statistics (New York: UN, 1979) Special Table C

Note: a. Excludes OPEC

Table 3.6 *Trade flows between developed and developing market economies in 1970 ($ bn)*

	LDC exports	LDC imports	Balance
SITC 1–4	17.15	6.48	10.67
SITC 5–9	8.49	33.52	−25.03

Source: *Yearbook of International Trade Statistics* (New York: UN, 1979) Special table C

3.4 are not gross distortions of reality. Note that the data in Table 3.6 remove intra-LDC and intra-DC trade, since Figure 3.4 relates to net rather than gross trade flows.

This general equilibrium analysis highlights the weakness of the employment displacement methodology that was criticised in Section I of this chapter. The effect of LDC industrialisation may be to contract overall DC–LDC trade, as Figure 3.4 demonstrates, instead of increasing it, as the displacement methodology takes for granted. Therefore partial and general equilibrium effects may be radically different.

A refinement of Table 3.6 is Table 3.7, which shows the composition of LDC imports of manufactures in gross and net terms. SITC 7 approximately corresponds with capital goods, and SITC 6 + 8 approximately corresponds with consumer goods. Table 3.7 shows that the structure of LDC imports of manufactures has been changing, with more weight attached to imports of capital goods. Figure 3.5 shows that since the late 1960s the growth of LDC imports of capital goods has risen in volume terms, both absolutely and relative to other categories of imports. In the light of the

Table 3.7 *Developing country imports: ratio of SITC 7 to SITC 6 + 8, 1960–78*

	Gross	Net (DC–LDC)
1960	1.0	1.12
1965	1.14	1.29
1970	1.27	1.47
1978	1.53	1.8

Source: *Yearbook of International Trade Statistics* (New York: UN, 1979)

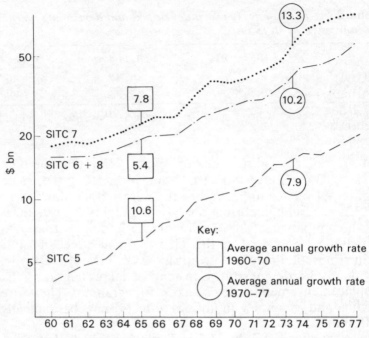

Figure 3.5   *The composition of developing countries' imports 1960–77 ($ bn at 1975 prices)*

arguments thus far, this phenomenon has two explanations:

(1) The thrust of LDC industrialisation has been towards the light rather than the heavy end of the spectrum of manufactures. This would have the effect of reducing the relative growth of imports in SITC 6 + 8 as LDCs become more self-sufficient.
(2) Because manufacturing output is most probably more capital intensive than LDC output as a whole, the relative growth of SITC 7 imports is likely to rise as LDCs industrialise. We shall return to this issue when describing Stage 4.

It is also worth pointing out how the terms of trade effects generated by LDC industrialisation relate to those identified by Prebisch (1964), who argued that there was a secular tendency for LDCs' terms of trade to move adversely. As was observed in Chapter 1, the relative price of primary products on world markets fell during the 1950s and 1960s. Prebisch's thesis has been criticised elsewhere, e.g. Flanders (1964) and we shall not consider the details of it here. Perhaps a more plausible version of his thesis was developed by Bhagwati (1958), who argued that LDC growth, if concentrated on the primary producing sector, could be economically immiserising. If, as experience suggests, the world income elasticity of demand for primary products is less than unity, an expansion of primary production would cause the relative price of primary products to fall on world markets and the terms of trade of primary producers such as LDCs to deteriorate. It is possible that the terms of trade loss to LDCs outweigh the benefits from primary growth. If so, growth is immiserising. At the very least the terms of trade loss offset some of the benefits of growth.

Figure 3.4 shows that by concentrating growth in the manufacturing sector the LDCs not only gain the direct benefits from this growth but they also secure terms of trade benefits, since the relative price of manufactures declines. This is the reverse implication of the immiserisation thesis; if primary production is disadvantageous then secondary production must be advantageous. By concentrating their development to a greater degree on manufacturing, the LDCs have turned the tide that was flowing against the relative price of primary products on world markets.

Stage 4: International Capital Flows

The debt problem of developing countries has become a major focus of attention. For example The Brandt Report and the 1981 *World Development Report* of the World Bank identify the LDC debt overhang as an issue that might jeopardise the stability of the international monetary system and hence the world economy as a whole. The fear is that LDC defaults on euro-currency loans will result in euro-bank failures, which in turn may topple the entire euro-currency banking pyramid. Since US, UK and other domestic banks hold euro-currency assets, a crash of the euro-currency system may contaminate domestic banking and monetary systems. At any rate, such is the fear. In principle euro-currency defaults are no different from defaults in the domestic banking sector which happen all the time. Defaults are an inevitable feature of financial markets, since we cannot avoid making bad loans some of the time (as long as we avoid making them most of the time). Therefore, the occasional euro-currency default should not be a major cause of concern. However, what is feared is a whole string of large defaults that would rock and even destroy present international financial institutions.

This pessimism assumes that LDC indebtedness is a disequilibrium phenomenon brought about by the OPEC oil price hikes. This may be so, and in the short term higher oil import bills seem likely to lead to greater indebtedness both for DCs and LDCs. What is more obscure is why higher oil prices should lead to permanent growth in indebtedness. If OPEC runs persistent current balance surpluses the rest of the world must run persistent capital account surpluses. However, the pessimistic view goes beyond this and maintains that even allowing for this LDC indebtedness is too large.

According to the Transition Theory, LDC indebtedness emerges as an equilibrium as opposed to a disequilibrium phenomenon; it is a natural implication of LDC industrialisation and as such it is not something to be feared. Instead it is something to be valued. The steady growth of LDC indebtedness is not brought about by oil prices (although they may be important in the short term) but by a fundamental realignment in the world capital market which reflects LDC industrialisation. In this realignment there has been an autonomous rise in the rate of return on capital in developing countries relative to the rate of return on capital in developed countries. This realignment generates a transfer of capital from DCs to LDCs in search of higher rates of return. Consequently, there is an export of capital from DCs to LDCs which is used to finance LDC industrialisation. Therefore LDC indebtedness plays a positive role in economic development. Moreover, in Chapter 6 it will be argued that this phenomenon has happened before in economic history without any of the consequences that are currently feared.

When considering Stage 1 we were unclear whether the roots of LDC industrialisation lay in shifts of the overall production function (λ_1), or whether they were unequally reflected in improvements in the productivity of labour and capital. Most probably all three phenomena were present. Whatever the case, the productivity of capital most probably improved, which is all we need to assume for our present purposes. What effect is an autonomous rise in the rate of return on LDC capital likely to have on the economies of the West? To answer this question we use Figure 3.6, which is based on the earlier analyses of MacDougall (1960) and Beenstock (1977). The left-hand sector shows the relationship between the marginal product of capital and the capital stock in developed countries, under the assumption that full employment prevails. The schedule is downward-sloping because of diminishing returns. Initially, i.e. before LDC industrialisation takes place, the capital stock is Oa so that the marginal product of capital is ae. GDP is therefore equal to A + B + C + D + E of which the labour share is A + B + E and the capital share (profits) is C + D.

In LDCs the initial relationship between the marginal product of capital and the stock of capital at given levels of employment is represented by the schedule Z_1. Initially, the LDC capital stock is Ob and the marginal produce of capital is bf. In Figure 3.6, bf = ae, because equilibrium in the world capital market requires that the rate of return on capital in

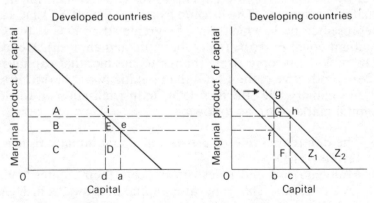

Figure 3.6 *Capital market equilibrium between developed and developing countries*

DCs must equal the rate of return on capital in LDCs, when allowance is made for relative capital risks. For presentational purposes we assume in Figure 3.6 that these relative risks net out to zero. If the rate of return on LDC capital were greater than its DC counterpart, investors and multinational companies would shift their capital from DCs to LDCs in search of higher returns and this process would narrow the differential rate of return. Capital movements cease only when rates of return have been equalised.

LDC industrialisation causes an autonomous increase in the rate of return on capital in the LDC capital market, i.e. a given capital stock is associated with a higher marginal product of capital. In Figure 3.6 this is represented by a rightward shift in the Z_1 schedule to Z_2. Thus given the initial LDC capital stock ob, the marginal product of capital rises by fg to bg. This means that the world capital market is no longer in equilibrium, since the rate of return on LDC capital at the margin is greater than the rate of return on DC capital. The world capital stock will tend to move from DCs to LDCs. In Figure 3.6, da = bc. Thus if da of the DC capital stock is reinvested in the LDC capital market, the marginal capital product in the DCs rises to di and the marginal capital product in the LDCs falls to ch from bg. Since ch = di, world capital market equilibrium has been restored.

GDP in developed countries falls by D + E; that is, profits fall by D and wages by E. The lower capital stock implies that real wages fall. The income from investments in LDCs is represented by F, which must be greater than D + E by an amount equal to 0.5 E (since bc = da and ch = di). Hence DC national income rises, thanks to the fact that capital is more productive in the LDCs than it initially was in the DCs.

In summary, the effects of LDC industrialisation on world capital markets are as follows:

- The differential rate of return on capital initially rises in favour of LDCs.
- Multinationals and investors relocate their capital from DCs to LDCs. This generates capital outflows from DCs to LDCs.
- The LDC capital account surplus is matched by a current

account deficit which reflects the import of capital goods from DCs as noted in Table 3.6 and in Figure 3.5.

● The return on DC capital tends to rise.
● GDP in DCs falls but national income rises.
● Wage rates in DCs fall.

It therefore follows that the LDCs must run current account deficits as an equilibrium phenomenon. If market . forces cause them to run capital account surpluses they must force them to run current account deficits. The capital account determines the current account. In contrast, the pessimistic view assumes that poor current account performance is causing LDCs to borrow more than is desirable, i.e. the current account drives the capital account. The Transition Theory thus reverses conventional views concerning causality.

In addition, as Lewis (1978a) has pointed out, industrialisation requires substantial investment in social capital. Inflows are not only induced by private investment but also by the substantial investment that is undertaken by governments in the provision of social overheads such as roads, hospitals, sewerage, water supply and all the other paraphernalia of urbanisation. The provision of these overheads is an integral part of the development process; they should not be regarded as unproductive extravagancies. Without them the return to private capital would be lower. Industrialisation and urbanisation have usually gone together, although in certain cases, for example, Taiwan, the rural sector has contributed directly to industrial growth. More typically, the pattern has been for the towns to attract the rural population into shanty towns which mushroom around the existing urban centres (such as in Manila, Abidjan, Rio de Janeiro, Jakarta). As the shanty populations settle themselves more permanently, enormous capital investment in social overheads is required. Lewis points out that there is nothing new about this phenomenon, it happened before with industrialisation in the US, West Germany and elsewhere.

TRANSNATIONAL COMPANIES
In the political economy of development there are few issues that arouse so much empassioned controversy as the role of

transnational or multinational corporations in DC–LDC economic relations. The Brandt Report devotes an entire chapter to these transnationals, and the United Nations has recently established a Center on Transnational Corporations. Marxists argue that the transnationals are vehicles for imperialism and that they have flouted the sovereignty of the Third World and exploited its economic resources. The Western economic establishment argues that the multinationals have been a vehicle for transmitting economic development and that without them LDC industrialisation would have been impossible. Figure 3.6 shows that multinational investment benefits LDC and DC interests. The transfer of capital generated an expansion of LDC income of F + G. F is repatriated to DCs as profits while G is retained in LDCs as wage income. Therefore the benefits are mutual.

In any case, multinationals' share of the LDC capital stock must be very small, as Table 3.8 suggests. In 1976 the ratio of the DC-owned capital stock in LDCs to LDC GDP was about 9 per cent. If the aggregate LDC capital : output ratio is assumed for arguments' sake to be 3, it follows that multinationals owned as little as 3 per cent of the LDC capital stock. Moreover, Table 3.8 suggests that this proportion has been declining. On the other hand, in certain countries and in certain industries transnational influence has been large. However, in the light of Table 3.8 this experience is not typical.

There is an important question: have transnationals themselves contributed to the outward shift in the relationship between the marginal capital product and the stock of capital in LDCs that was represented in Figure 3.6? Or have

Table 3.8 *Multinationals' share of LDC capital stock 1967–76 (bn)*

	1 *Private inward direct investment position in LDCs*	2 *GDP in developing market economies*	*1 ÷ 2 (%)*
1967	35.1	270	13.0
1976	84.4	947	8.9

Sources: 1. Billerbeck and Yasugi (1979) Table S1.9 for DAC countries
2. *Statistical Yearbook* (New York: UN) various issues

they only responded to a shift that occurred independently of their behaviour? Most probably they contributed as well as responded, especially in terms of the transfer of technology and business know-how. In this context we may draw on Vernon's (1966) product cycle thesis and relate it to transnational involvement in the LDCs. According to Vernon the product cycle has three stages:

(1) A new product is developed for the home market in, say, the United States. Comparative advantage is less important than being in direct contact with the fledgling market so that the product can be modified and adapted to market needs. In this stage the product is not standardised and any surplus production is exported, although the export market is not exploited.

(2) The product has established itself in the home market, and some overseas markets begin to develop. Product standardisation also begins to develop. Marketing advantages cause outward investment so that the product can be supplied locally in overseas markets.

(3) The product is completely standardised and marketing methods are fully established. At this point comparative advantage takes over, and multinationals set up supply bases in LDCs, especially in the case of labour intensive products.

No doubt the product cycle has contributed to multinational activity in LDCs, as with Zeiss in South-east Asia for instance, and Volkswagen in Brazil. But it does not suggest a sudden increase in this involvement, since the product cycle has always existed and is not a new phenomenon. If, however, LDC industrialisation is autonomous, as has been argued in this chapter, Stage 3 of the product cycle will begin to apply to LDCs and the backlog of mature products will become candidates for transnational investment in LDCs. This is the implication of the Transition Theory.

Stage 5: The Mismatch Hypothesis

Thus far nothing has been said about unemployment or recession in relation to the Transition Theory. On the contrary, the analysis of Figures 3.3, 3.4 and 3.6 assumed full employment in the developed countries. The purpose of this assumption was to show the equilibrium effects of LDC industrialisation, i.e. where the world economy is heading once labour, capital and product markets have fully adjusted. It may, however, be several years before these adjustments are complete and so a disequilibrium theory is necessary. The mismatch hypothesis is a subset of the Transition Theory and is concerned with the adjustment process between equilibria in the world economy.

The basic insight of this hypothesis is illustrated by Figure 3.7, which repeats the right-hand sector of Figure 3.6. The initial equilibrium production point in developed countries is a, along the DC production possibility frontier (TT). LDC industrialisation causes this equilibrium to move from a to d, i.e. if capital and labour markets are perfectly flexible resources will immediately shift from the manufacturing sector to the non-manufacturing sector, so that one day a is produced and the next day d is produced. Labour and capital remain fully employed; they simply change what they are producing overnight.

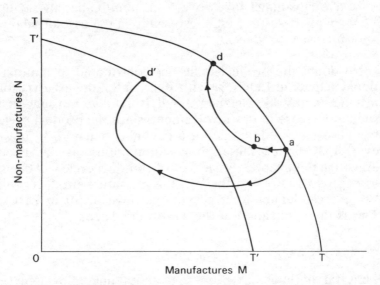

Figure 3.7 *The mismatch hypothesis*

This idealised world is unlikely to apply, for many reasons. Instead of resources jumping from one sector to the next, they are more likely to adjust more slowly. As the demand for M falls, manufacturing output is likely to fall at first without any increase in the output of N. After some time, however, resources begin to relocate in the non-manufacturing sector. In Figure 3.7 we assume that M initially falls by ba before non-manufacturing output begins to expand. Eventually the resources released from the manufacturing sector find their way into the non-manufacturing sector and equilibrium is achieved at d. Therefore the disequilibrium production possibility frontier is abd and lies inside the equilibrium production possibility frontier.

Along abd there is a mismatch between the demand for resources and their supply. Demand conditions require the non-manufacturing sector to expand and the manufacturing sector to contract. However, supply conditions resist this change, because factor markets are assumed to operate sluggishly. Recession therefore builds up in the manufacturing sector while the non-manufacturing sector booms. The economy is thus affected by boom and slump at the same time.

Mismatch may manifest itself even within the manufacturing sector. Under Stage 4 it was argued that LDC industrialisation tends to trigger a change in the composition of international trade in manufactures. The LDCs export light manufactures and import capital goods which their industrialisation requires. Hence the composition of DC manufactured exports becomes more weighted in favour of capital goods. Resources, however, may not be perfectly mobile within the manufacturing sector and mismatch unemployment will tend to emerge.

Mismatch problems are essentially transitory. The Transition Theory does not imply that LDC industrialisation causes permanent unemployment. On the contrary, full employment is eventually achieved at d on Figure 3.7. Mismatch is a consequence of sluggish adjustment which, in the nature of things, is temporary. Also, it is misleading to argue that the LDCs cause even temporary unemployment in DCs, since it is a reflection of sluggish factor markets. The LDCs are simply one irritant among many others, such as technological change; the basic problem is the sluggishness of factor markets.

If, as Stage 4 suggests, the DC capital stock falls, the production possibility frontier will shrink to T^1T^1. The larger proportionate fall along the M axis reflects the judgement that manufactures are relatively capital intensive. At d^1 the slope of T^1T^1 is the same as the slope of TT at d; therefore it is the new equilibrium. The disequilibrium production possibility frontier is ad^1 which shows that both M and N may fall.

At d we know from Figure 3.3 that real wages are higher. In this case real wage stickiness cannot be the cause of unemployment. Instead unemployment reflects mismatch. At d^1 real wages are likely to be lower than a. On the one hand, the lower capital stock reduces real wages. On the other, the rise in N/M raises the real wage along the lines of the Stolper–Samuelson theorem. However, the former effect is likely to dominate, in which case real wages must fall. If they do not fall sufficiently classical unemployment will emerge, as well as mismatch unemployment.

Mismatch problems have numerous causes. First, both human and physical capital are putty-clay, i.e. there are costs of adjustment in factor deployment. Steelworkers have to retrain for jobs in the non-manufacturing sector, they cannot switch effortlessly from one job to the next. Likewise physical capital that is no longer required in one sector of the economy cannot simply be transferred to other sectors where capital requirements may be different. Some capital equipment may have to be scrapped because the costs of adaptation are too high. The same applies to human capital; costs of retraining for workers in their fifties may be too high.

Secondly, restrictive practices in labour markets may prevent the redeployment of labour. Trade unions may pressurise firms to stay in business rather than encourage their members to adapt to the changing economic environment. Sometimes management gangs up with its employees to force governments to limit imports from LDCs, provide subsidies, etc.

Thirdly, there may be a geographical dimension to mismatch. The new jobs may be in different parts of the country. Labour mobility may be impeded by inefficient housing markets. For example, in the UK a third of all housing is in the local authority sector where housing is rationed at fixed prices which are heavily subsidised. There is a great disincentive for workers in such housing to relocate, since they will either lose the subsidy or go to the bottom of a housing list elsewhere in the country. Indeed, this hypothesis has been corroborated by Hughes and McKormick (1981), who find that labour mobility has been adversely affected by arrangements in the market for accommodation.

Stage 6: Equilibrium

The last stage in the Transition Theory is the new steady-state in which factor markets have adjusted to LDC industrialisation. There is little to say about this stage since we have described it by implication under the descriptions of the five previous stages. It would be wrong, however, to imply that LDC industrialisation happens once-and-for-all. We have assumed this for heuristic purposes. In 1979 the world population was 4.3 billion and was distributed as shown on Table 3.9. The Third World consists of 75 per cent of the world's population and the majority of LDC industrialisation thus far has been concentrated in the middle income developing countries, especially the newly industrialising countries (NICs). This implies that all that we have so far seen is the thin end of the wedge, for in the fullness of time economic development is likely to embrace all of the

Table 3.9 *Distribution of world population in 1979 (%)*

Low-income developing countries	52.6
Middle-income developing countries	22.9
Newly-industrialising countries[a]	7.3
Industrial market economies	15.6
Capital-surplus oil exporters	0.6
Non-market industrial economies	8.3

Note: a. Defined in OECD (1979) as Greece, Portugal, Spain, Yugoslavia, Brazil, Mexico, Hong Kong, Korea, Singapore and Taiwan

world's population. It has taken 200 years for about 30 per cent of the global population to be affected. We cannot extrapolate from this experience to conclude that it will take another six or seven centuries for the remaining 70 per cent to be changed. Improved communications and the accumulation of experience point to an acceleration in this process. The General Conference of UNIDO in 1975 adopted the Lima Declaration which included the target share of LDCs in world manufacturing to reach at least 25 per cent by the year 2000 (allowing for the centrally planned economies, in 1980 it was 11 per cent). These declarations are meaningless. Nevertheless it is arguable that the LDC bandwagon is rolling; the present generation of NICs will be succeeded by another generation, and so on. During the 1960s and 1970s it was the turn of some of the South-east Asian and Latin American countries. During the 1980s and 1990s the initiative may pop up elsewhere. If this is so, the equilibrium for the DCs may be troubled, since they will have to adjust constantly to LDC industrialisation. What we have seen thus far may be no more than a beginning.

Appendix

Multisectoral Models

In the main text of this chapter a simple textbook 2×2 model was proposed in which there were two factors of production and two outputs. This had the advantage of simplicity, so that a number of fairly complex general equilibrium exercises could be carried out graphically. Another advantage was familiarity with the 2×2 model since it is so standard. It is well known that in more general models almost anything can happen and numerous, though plausible, restrictions would be necessary to generate the Transition Theory. Nevertheless the simple 2×2 model most probably carries 95 per cent of the basic insights and it should be judged on these practical criteria.

In a more complicated model we would wish to add at least two further dimensions. First, the LDCs and DCs will have a non-traded goods sector (N). Clearly, developments in this sector in the LDCs could only exert an indirect influence on the DCs and vice versa via relative price movements. Secondly, it might be sensible to disaggregate manufactures into advanced manufactures (M_a) and less sophisticated manufactures (M_s) and to assume that the DCs have a comparative advantage in the former and the LDCs a comparative advantage in the latter. In this way the initial trading situation has two-way trade in manufactures, with the DCs importing M_s from the LDCs and the LDCs importing M_a from the DCs. These complications imply a four-sector output model based on A, M_a and N, which we denote by Q_i (i = 1, . . .4) and their associated prices by P_i. Q_{ij} is the output of i in the jth region where j = 1, 2, for DCs and LDCs respectively. A denotes primary production. In total there are eight (ij) production functions

$$Q = F_{ij}(K_{ij}^+, L_{ij}^+)$$

where the factor supply constraints are

$$\sum_i K_{ij} = K_j$$

$$\sum_i L_{ij} = L_j$$

There are eight first order conditions

$$P_{ij} \frac{\partial F_{ij}}{\partial K_{ij}} = r_j, \qquad P_{ij} \frac{\partial F_{ij}}{\partial L_{ij}} = w_j$$

where r and w are the cost of capital and the wage rate respectively. Assuming factor immobility r_1 and r_2 are not directly related, nor are w_1 and w_2. But free trade requires that $P_{i1} = P_{i2}$ i = 1, . . . , 3. For given P_{ij} the model solves for the ten unknowns K_{ij}, L_{ij}, r_j and w_j. In turn on the basis of K_{ij} and L_{ij} we may solve for Q_{ij} via the production functions.

P_{ij} are determined by the following set of market equilibrium conditions

$$\sum_j Q_{ij} = \sum_j Q_{ij}^d \qquad i = 1, \ldots, 3$$

where Q_{ij}^d denotes the demand schedule for Q_{ij} and are of the form

$$Q_{ij}^d = D_{ij}(\overset{+}{Q}_j, \overline{P}_{ij}, \overset{+}{P}_{kj}) \qquad k \neq i$$

The equilibrium conditions for non-traded goods are

$$Q_{4j} = Q_{4j}^d$$

i.e. supply has to be consumed domestically. Thus we have five market conditions that solve for P_{ij} ($i = 1, \ldots, 3$) and P_{4j} ($j = 1, 2$).

The condition for balanced trade for region j is

$$\sum_{i=1}^{3} (Q_{ij}^D - Q_{ij})P_i = 0$$

which, if not satisfied, implies an exchange rate adjustment that will feed around the entire model.

In the main text we assumed that $i = 1, 2$, and that all goods are traded. In this simple case the Stolper–Samuelson theorem may be stated as follows. The wage share is

$$\frac{w}{r} = S = \frac{Y_i - K_i F_{iK}}{F_{iK} L_i}$$

The total differential of S with respect to say P_1 is

$$\frac{dS}{dP_1} = \frac{F_{1K}L_1\left(\dfrac{dY_1}{dP_1} - K_1\dfrac{dF_{1K}}{dP_1} - F_{1K}\dfrac{dK_1}{dP_1}\right) - \left(Y_1 - K_1F_{1K}\right)\left(L_1\dfrac{dF_{1K}}{dP_1} + F_{1K}\dfrac{dL_1}{dP_1}\right)}{(F_{1K}K_1)^2}$$

The numerator may be expressed as

$$\frac{1}{F_{1K}}\frac{dF_{1K}}{dP_1} - \frac{1}{Y_1}\frac{dY_1}{dP_1} + \frac{1}{L_1}\frac{dL_1}{dP_1}\left(1 - \frac{K_1F_{1K}}{Y_1}\right)$$

$$+ \frac{K_1}{Y_1}\frac{F_{1K}}{K_1}\frac{dK_1}{dP_1} = \frac{1}{F_{1K}}\frac{dF_{1K}}{dP_1}$$

since via the production function

$$\frac{1}{Y_1} \frac{dY_1}{dP_1} = \left(1 - \frac{K_1 F_{1K}}{Y_1}\right) \frac{1}{L_1} \frac{dL_1}{dP_1} + \frac{K_1 F_{1K}}{Y_1 K_1} \frac{dK_1}{dP_1}$$

Thus the sign of dS/dP_1 depends on the sign of dF_{1K}/dP_1, according to the Stolper–Samuelson theorem.

The Rybczynski theorem may be expressed in terms of the effect of an increase in K upon r. Since

$$r = F_{1K}(K_1, L_1)$$

$$\frac{dr}{dK} = \frac{dF_{1K}}{dK} = \frac{\partial F_{1K}}{\partial K_1} \frac{dK_1}{dK} + \frac{\partial F_{1K}}{\partial L_1} \frac{dL_1}{dK}$$

$$= \frac{\partial F_{1K}}{\partial K_1} \left(\frac{dK_1 - dL_1}{dK}\right)$$

since

$$\frac{\partial F_{1K}}{\partial K_1} = - \frac{\partial F_{1K}}{\partial L_1}$$

If Y_1 is capital intensive $dK_1 > dL_1$, so that $dr/dK < 0$.

The issue is, how do these results translate to the more complicated model? Kemp (1969) shows that both where there are more products than factors and where there are non-traded goods the analysis becomes extremely complicated, and concludes that nothing *a priori* can be deduced. In our model both these cases apply. Nevertheless for the results of the 2×2 model to carry over it would be intuitively necessary to make the following assumptions:

- F_{11} and F_{31} are labour intensive, i.e. DC imports are labour intensive while F_{21} is capital intensive.
- F_{41} is labour intensive relative to F_{21}, so that as Q_{41} rises relative to Q_{21} r_1 tends to fall relative to w_1.

- $$\frac{dP_2}{d(P_1/P_3)} < 0, \qquad \frac{dQ_{41}}{d(P_1/P_3)} > 0$$

i.e. the price of advanced manufactures falls when the price of primary products rises relative to the price of simple manufactures and non-traded output rises in the DCs. The former assumption implies that the elasticity of substitution in demand between manufactures is high. Thus as P_3 falls Q_2^d falls sharply driving down P_2. The second assumption is related to this: since P_3 has fallen the production of non-tradeables becomes more profitable.

These and their derivative assumptions seem plausible enough but it would be a thankless task to thrash out the complex restrictions on the F_{ii} and the D_{ij}, although this is possible. In fact, the model could be further complicated by incorporating variable factor supplies, e.g. the supply of capital depends on the price of capital and the supply of labour depends on real wage rates. Furthermore the factor markets could be integrated between the DCs and the LDCs. But it should go without saying that the *a priori* analysis of such models would be more or less fruitless in the absence of strong prior assumptions about the nature of the model.

4

Empirical Aspects of the Transition Theory

This chapter explores the empirical foundations of the Transition Theory over the period 1950–80. Chapter 6 will apply the Transition Theory to the relationship between Britain, as the archetypal industrialised country, and the latter-day NICs of the US, Germany, Russia, etc., over the period 1850–1913. For the moment, however, we are concerned with the empirical relationship between LDC industrialisation and economic recession in the OECD as a whole in the light of the Transition Theory. It is argued that the facts broadly fit the deductions of the theory in every respect. The surge in LDC industrialisation that began in the mid-1960s triggered a sequence of global economic adjustments in the following fifteen years that has underpinned the protracted recession in the bloc of industrialised countries.

Section I examines the Transition Theory using informal empirical methods. That is, the data that are pertinent to the theory are analysed by eye rather than by formal statistical methods. In Section II some more formal econometric results are reported.

I Informal Data Analysis

In this section each stage of the Transition Theory is considered in turn. (The stages were described in detail in Chapter 3.)

Stage 1: LDC Growth

Figure 4.1 records what was already observed in Chapter 1. Since the vertical axis measures the natural log of GDP at 1975 prices the slope of the graph measures the exponential rate of growth. For the developing countries this rate of growth rises from about 1967. The dotted line extrapolates the trend rate of growth that was observed over the period 1950–67. This clearly demonstrates that LDC growth has been more buoyant since the second half of the 1960s. Moreover, this buoyancy has persisted through the vicissitudes of the 1970s.

Whereas LDC growth accelerates after 1967 the reverse applies to the developed countries. Figure 4.1 shows the trend line based on the period 1958–69, over which growth was rapid. This suggests that DC growth has had three trend phases in the postwar period: 1950–8, 1958–69 and 1969–78. The middle phase was unprecedented, as noted in Chapter 1. While the first and last phases rank fairly well in terms of a broader historical perspective, the implication of the Transition Theory is that the break in the DC trend after 1969 is related to the break in the LDC trend two years before.

Figure 4.2 plots the share of manufactures in LDC output. In terms of Figure 3.1, industrialisation is accompanied by a

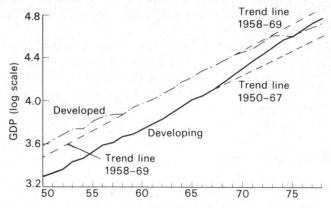

Source: *Yearbook of National Accounts* (New York: UN) various issues

Figure 4.1 *GDP in developed and developing market economies 1950–78 (at 1975 prices)*

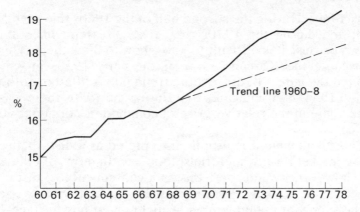

Source: *Handbook of World Development Statistics* (New York: UN) 1979

Figure 4.2 *Share of manufacturing output in developing country GDP 1960–78 (at 1975 prices)*

rise in this ratio. Figure 4.2 shows that this ratio had been rising during the early 1960s; indeed it had been rising at a more or less constant rate since 1948. An extrapolation of this trend beyond 1968 records an increase in the rate at which this ratio increased during the second half of the 1960s. Thus we may conclude:

- During the second half of the 1960s LDC growth increased from about 4.8 per cent p.a. over the period 1950–65 to over 6 per cent p.a.
- This was accompanied by an increase in the share of manufactures in total output. By the early 1970s this amounted to more than one per cent of LDC output, an increase which previously took five years to accomplish.
- By the end of the 1960s DC economic growth began to decline.

Stage 2: World Prices

The next step in our investigation is to determine the effect of the disturbances of Stage 1 on the structure of world relative prices. Figure 4.3 plots the ratio of world commodity prices to the world price of manufactures. It shows that the relative price of commodities fell during the 1950s and the early 1960s. During the second half of the 1960s they stabilised, and during the 1970s they rose. No trend lines are drawn because it is difficult to know how to draw them. This is because the Korean boom of the early 1950s grossly inflated the index. If, however, a trend line is fitted over the period 1954–64 it indicates that during the 1970s there was an increase in the relative price of commodities of about 50 per cent.

This phenomenon is usually interpreted as a disturbance in the market for raw materials, food, etc. In terms of Figure 3.2, however, we interpret this as a consequence of disturbances in the market for manufactures. The autonomous rise in the supply of manufactures brought about under Stage 1 results in a fall in the relative price of manufactures on world markets. Figure 4.3 seems to suggest that the change in price relativities occurred a year or two too soon. In the light of what occurred under Stage 1 the change should have occurred during the second half of the 1960s. However, it is difficult to disentangle secular from cyclical movements in the index. The buoyant state of the world economy in the mid-1960s in any case caused the index to rise. When the subsequent recession came the index did not fall as far as might have been expected. Therefore Figure 4.3 does not necessarily imply discrepancies in timing.

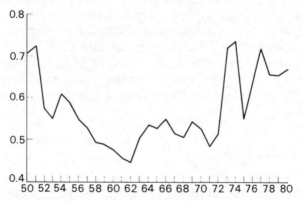

Source: Monthly Bulletin of Statistics (New York: UN) various issues

Figure 4.3   The ratio of the UN commodity price index to the UN index of world price of manufactures exports 1950–80

Figure 4.4 shows that in the early 1960s LDC terms of trade had been declining sharply, the continuation of a trend that had emerged in the 1950s. Because, as Table 3.6 indicates, LDCs are primarily exporters of primary products and importers of manufactures, the terms of trade index should be positively correlated with the relative commodity price index of Figure 4.3. Indeed, Figure 4.4 shows that the secular deterioration in the terms of trade began to be arrested in 1966, stabilized during the rest of the decade and rose in the early 1970s. This chart is not continued beyond 1972 since the data become distorted by the OPEC oil price hikes. Nevertheless, it is clear that there is a favourable structural

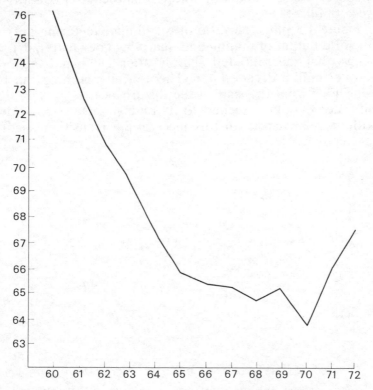

Source: *Handbook of World Development Statistics* (New York: UN) various
issues

Figure 4.4   *Commodity terms of trade of developing market economies 1960–72*

break in LDCs' terms of trade. This break coincides with the relative fall in the world price of manufactures. The timing of the break also fits with the Transition Theory, since theoretically it should have taken place during the second half of the 1960s, which was indeed the case.

The fact that LDC industrialisation is concentrated in the manufacturing sector does not necessarily mean that for the world as a whole the relative supply of manufactures rises. It was argued in relation to Figure 3.2 that the opposite might even happen, especially if the relative demand for manufactures is price inelastic and if the income elasticity of demand for manufactures by LDCs is less than unity or small. Figures 4.5 and 4.6 indicate that the latter conditions were fulfilled.

Figure 4.5 plots the ratio of world manufacturing output to world output of mining and quarrying (raw materials). It shows that the ratio fell sharply after 1967 and did not recover until a decade later. Theoretically, nothing can be concluded from the sign of the disturbance. However, significance may be attached to its timing, since it coincides with the relative price disturbances, as the Transition Theory

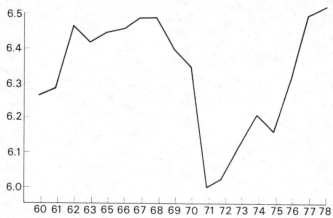

Source: Handbook of World Development Statistics (New York: UN) various issues

Figure 4.5   *The ratio of world* manufacturing output to output of mining and quarrying 1960–78 (at 1975 $)*

Note: *Excludes centrally planned economies

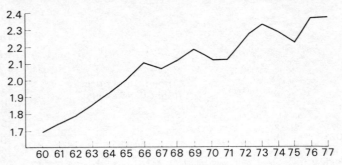

Source: *Handbook of World Development Statistics* (New York: UN) various issues

Figure 4.6 *The ratio of world* manufacturing output to output of mining, quarrying and agriculture 1960–77 (at 1975 $)*

Note: *Excludes centrally planned economies

predicts. Thus once more the second half of the 1960s emerges as a flashpoint in the world economy.

Figure 4.6 plots the ratio of world manufacturing production to world primary production. The ratio had been steadily rising during the early 1960s. However, after 1966 this rise was checked and a new, less progressive trend emerges. This transformation is not as pronounced as that shown in Figure 4.5 but the qualitative change is the same and the timing accords with the Transition Theory.

The relative price of services in the DCs is plotted in Figure 4.7. Two versions are presented: the ratio of service prices to industrial prices, and the ratio of service prices to the GDP deflator. Since in Chapter 3 the relationship between relative service prices and relative manufactures prices was not explicitly discussed, it will be examined now. We assume the economy consists of primary, secondary and tertiary sectors, whose product prices are denoted P_1, P_2 and P_3. Relative supply and demand depends on the structure of relative prices. For example, the relative supply of manufactures (secondary production) is assumed to vary directly with the price of manufactures relative to primary and tertiary prices:

$$S_2 = \alpha_1 \frac{P_2}{P_1} + \alpha_2 \frac{P_2}{P_3}$$

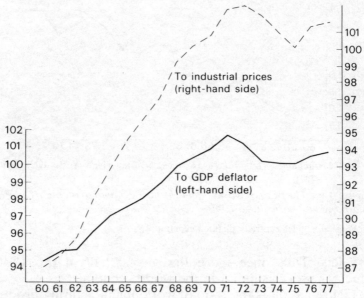

Source: *Handbook of World Development Statistics* (New York: UN) various issues

Figure 4.7   *The relative price of services in Developed Market Economies 1960–77 (1975 = 100)*

The relative demand for manufactures varies inversely with these relative prices:

$$D_2 = -\beta_1 \frac{P_2}{P_1} - \beta_2 \frac{P_2}{P_3}$$

In equilibrium relative supply must equal relative demand, in which case the relationship between these relative prices is:

$$\frac{P_2}{P_3} = -\frac{(\alpha_1 + \beta_1)P_2}{(\alpha_2 + \beta_2)P_1}$$

Therefore a fall in the price of manufactures relative to primary products (i.e. a fall in P_2/P_1) brings about a rise in the relative price of manufactures relative to services (i.e. a rise in P_2/P_3).

Figure 4.7 shows that during the 1960s the relative price of services was rising. This steady increase was reversed in the early 1970s, but the rate of increase began to falter in 1968. According to the Transition Theory, P_3/P_2 should have fallen from what otherwise would have been the case, because P_2/P_1 fell (Figure 4.3). Therefore both the timing and the nature of the change in relative service prices seems to support the Transition Theory.

Stage 3: De-Industrialisation in the West

Under this stage several related phenomena must be examined. These are:

(1)   The share of secondary output in total DC output which the Transition Theory implies should fall.
(2)   The profit share in DCs which the Transition Theory implies should fall under the assumptions made in Chapter 3.
(3)   The changing pattern in DC–LDC trade relationships with regard to:

(a)   the rise in LDC share of manufactured trade,
(b)   the growth of intra-LDC trade relative to DC–LDC trade, and
(c)   the changing composition of LDC manufactured imports in favour of capital goods.

(1)   OUTPUT

Figure 4.8 plots the shares of industrial and manufacturing output in total DC output. In both cases the share rose steadily throughout most of the 1960s, continuing a trend that emerged during the 1950s, although with somewhat greater force. After 1966 this trend begins to falter. The industrial production share more or less stops in its tracks, while the manufacturing share loses momentum although it still continues to rise. The oil shock of 1973–4 reverses both shares, as suggested in Chapter 2. A similar story is told by Figure 4.9, which plots industry's share of total employment in OECD countries. The relative growth of the industrial and manufacturing sectors was checked precisely at the time that the Transition Theory indicates.

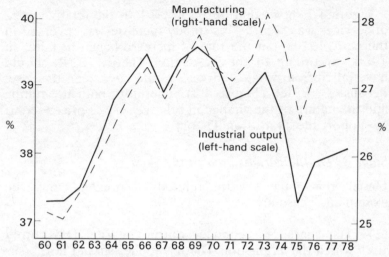

Source: *Handbook of World Development Statistics* (New York: UN) 1979

Figure 4.8   *The shares of output in GDP of developed market economies 1960–78 (at 1975 prices)*

Thus the de-industrialisation process began well before the OPEC oil price hikes and the explosion of commodity prices in the early 1970s. Instead it coincided with LDC industrialisation and the change in the structure of world relative prices. It is sometimes argued, e.g. by Bacon and

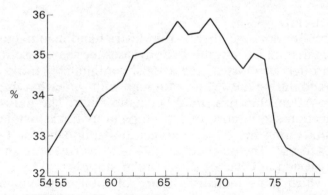

Source: *OECD Labour Force Statistics*

Figure 4.9   *Industry's share of total employment in developed countries 1954–80.*

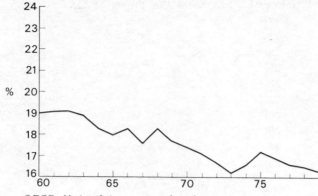

Source: OECD, National Accounts, various issues

Figure 4.10   *The share of government consumption in OECD GDP 1960–79 (at 1975 prices)*

Eltis (1980), that the roots of de-industrialisation lie in the growth of public expenditure. If the public sector increases its claim on economic resources, de-industrialisation as measured here will occur for two reasons. First, arithmetically the industrial production ratio must decline if the public expenditure ratio is to rise. Secondly, the higher taxation or increased government borrowing that is necessitated by the increase in public expenditure will adversely affect the supply side of the economy. While the Bacon–Eltis thesis might apply to the British economy, Figure 4.10 implies that it certainly does not apply across the OECD as a whole, because proportionate government expenditure has been declining since 1960. In this respect the second half of the 1960s is typical of the 1960s and 1970s as a whole. Therefore we cannot look to the Bacon–Eltis thesis to account for the onset of de-industrialisation in the second half of the 1960s. Only the Transition Theory seems to provide an explanation for both the timing of events and the nature of these events.

(2) PROFITS

Figure 4.11 plots the pre-tax profit share based on a weighted average of nine major OECD countries. The weights reflect GDP shares in 1970 and refer to the industrial and transportation sectors. The trend line shows that during the second half of the 1960s the profit share began to decline at

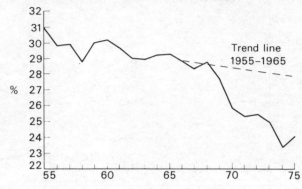

Figure 4.11　*The share of profits in GDP for developed countries 1955–75*

a time and in a direction that is consistent with the Transition Theory. By implication the wage share rose. The latter development has always puzzled economic analysts and it is sometimes argued that increased trade union militancy was responsible. The events in France in May 1968 are usually cited, but this clearly cannot explain developments in other OECD countries. In any case, economic theory does not automatically imply that trade union militancy increases the wage share in the medium term.

Even if the militancy theory is accepted another theory is required to explain the rise of militancy in the first place. In so far as the Transition Theory is valid, militancy could have been brought about by the reallocation of resources in favour of relatively labour-intensive activities while de-industrialisation takes place. That is, the de-industrialisation that is triggered by LDC industrialisation raises the demand for labour in the DCs and provides labour with the market power to behave more militantly. Therefore the wage explosion which took place at the end of the 1960s across OECD countries as a whole was an implication of the Transition Theory. Trade union power is always circumscribed by market forces.

Notice that this argument turns on its head the more familiar claim that LDC industrialisation is undermining DC jobs and therefore trade union power. As always in economic analysis, it is necessary to look beyond the direct effects and immediate consequences of events. The Transition Theory implies that LDC industrialisation shifts the balance of market power away from capital in favour of labour.

(3) TRADE

Table 3.5 supported the deduction of the Transition Theory that overall DC–LDC trade is likely to contract as the differences in comparative advantage narrow. Table 3.7 confirmed the prediction that the structure of LDC manufactured imports became more capital intensive. Table 4.1 shows that LDC trade grew faster than LDC–DC trade after 1968, so that not only did LDCs capture markets in the DCs but they also captured third markets and subsequently more of their own trade. Exports of manufactures to DCs grew from 9.8 per cent p.a. in the 1960s to more than 11 per cent p.a. in the 1970s. Intra-LDC trade in manufactures also grew faster, but by a much larger amount: the growth rate rose from 9 per cent p.a. to about 15%. Notice that in the second period total exports to DCs grew more slowly, supporting the trade contraction thesis to which references has already been made.

Although Table 4.1 indicates an increased emphasis on intra-LDC trade in manufactures after 1968, Figure 4.12 suggests a rather different story. According to this chart, the share of intra-LDC trade in manufactures fell steadily between 1963 and 1973, although the rate of decline abated to some extent after 1968 and stabilised after 1973. Whereas Table 4.1 implies that LDCs did not particularly target their manufactured exports on industrialised countries, the opposite is implied by Figure 4.12 which implies that manu-

Table 4.1 *Geographical distribution of LDC exports 1960–78 (growth rates p.a. at 1970 prices)*

	To DCs		To LDCs	
	Total	SITC 5 – 8	Total	SITC 5 – 8
1960–68	6.3	9.8	5.1	9.0
1968–78	5.0	11.2	8.0	14.7

Source: Monthly Bulletin of Statistics (New York: UN, July 1980) Special table F

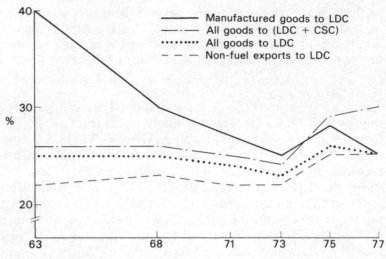

Source: Havrylyshn and Wolf (1982)

Figure 4.12   *The share of developing countries' exports going to developing countries 1963–77*

factured export growth was heavily but not exclusively concentrated on DC markets.

The reason for this difference is that in Figure 4.12 manufactures are defined net of SITC 68 (processed ferrous metals), whereas the UN data in Table 4.1 includes SITC 68 within the group SITC 5–8. This underscores the need to disaggregate between different commodity groupings, although both data sources suggest that proportionate intra-LDC exports of manufactures strengthened in relation to previous trends during the 1970s.

The rise in the importance of LDCs in world trade in manufactures may be clearly seen in Figure 4.13. In the space of a decade LDCs doubled their market share, and the latest indication is that the LDCs are relentlessly increasing their share. The important thing to notice is that the growth in market share accelerates during the second half of the 1960s, reflecting the developments already observed in relation to Figures 4.1 and 4.2.

This growth also reflects the developments recorded in Figure 4.14 which plots the LDC's share of world manufacturing value-added and GDP. Both of these shares were

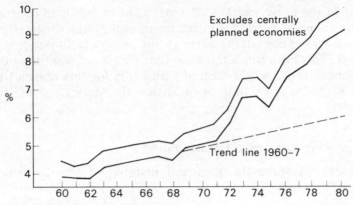

Source: UNIDO (1981) p. 36

Figure 4.13 *The developing countries' share of world trade in manufactures 1960–80 (at 1975 prices)*

stationary until 1967. After this, however, they rose sharply. Therefore as LDCs increased their share of world economic activity they also increased their share of world trade. The reason why the centrally planned economies are excluded from Figure 4.14 is that their trade and output shares are unrelated. Their trade share for manufactures fell from 13 per

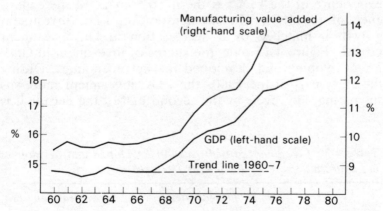

Sources: UNIDO (1981) p. 29; *Compendium of World Development Indicators* (New York: UN) 1979
Note: 'world' excludes centrally planned economies

Figure 4.14 *The developing countries' share of world output 1960–80 (at 1975 prices)*

cent in the early 1960s to 8.1 per cent in 1980. In contrast their share of world manufacturing value added rose from about 15 per cent in the early 1960s to almost 24 per cent in 1980. This underlines the view that CPEs are not fully integrated into the world economy and it is for this reason that we sometimes exclude them from the definition of 'the world'.

Stage 4: International Capital Flows

Under this stage the principal insights of the Transition Theory were:

(1)   LDC investment rises,
(2)   DC investment falls,
(3)   DC capital flows to LDCs rise, and
(4)   the LDC debt 'problem' is an equilibrium phenomenon and is thus not a problem at all, by and large.

(1)   LDC INVESTMENT GROWTH
Gross domestic fixed capital formation in LDCs accelerated during the second half of the 1960s. The average annual growth rates in investment are shown on Table 4.2. The experience of the LDCs is the mirror image of the experience of the DCs. The acceleration in LDC investment growth is matched by a deceleration in DC investment growth. Figure 4.15 plots the shares of investment in GDP for developing and developed market economies. During the early part of the 1960s the LDC investment ratio was stagnating. However, by the second half of the decade it is

Table 4.2   *Investment growth rates in developed and developing countries 1960–77 (% p.a. at 1975 prices)*

	Developing countries	Developed countries
1960–65	5.2	7.1
1965–70	7.8	5.3
1970–77	10.7	1.2

Source: *Handbook of World Development Statistics* (New York: UN) 1979

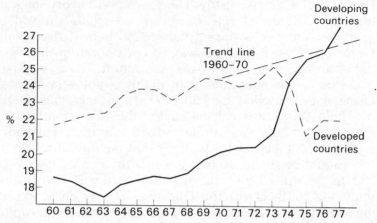

Source: *Handbook of World Development Statistics* (New York: UN) 1979

Figure 4.15   *Share of investment in GDP in developed and developing countries 1960–77 (at 1975 prices)*

clear that a sustained rising trend in the ratio had taken root. Thereafter the investment ratio begins to rise in an almost exponential fashion. By the mid-1970s the LDC ratio overtook the DC investment ratio.

In the DCs the investment ratio grew steadily during the 1960s, continuing a trend that began in the mid-1950s. However, the trend line shows that the growth in the investment ratio began to run out of steam around 1970. The collapse in the investment ratio in 1974–5 was no doubt a consequence of the OPEC oil price hikes.

As far as the Transition Theory is concerned, the central characteristic of these data is the strengthening of LDC investment behaviour during the second half of the 1960s and the weakening in DC investment behaviour at the turn of the decade. This suggests that there was a delay of about two years before DC investment began to react to the re-alignment in international capital markets.

(2) INTERNATIONAL RATES OF RETURN

The acceleration of LDC investment was accompanied by capital inflows from DCs. Ideally it would be desirable to show the behaviour of the rates of return to capital in the

DCs and LDCs respectively. The Transition Theory suggests that the differential rate of return on capital moved in favour of the LDCs during the second half of the 1960s. Unfortunately we have no way of corroborating this since the necessary data do not exist. We can, however, evaluate one side of the equation, even if this is not very helpful. Using data compiled by Hill (1979), an aggregate GDP-weighted series was calculated for the rate of return on capital based on several industrialised countries. This index is plotted on Figure 4.16. It shows that the rate of return on DC capital began to decline towards the end of the 1960s and fell sharply during the first half of the 1970s. If anything, this conflicts with the Transition Theory since, according to Figure 3.6 the increase in the rate of return on capital in the LDCs should drive up the rate of return on capital in the DCs. More likely the decline in the DC rate of return reflects some of the considerations raised in Chapter 2 to which it should be remembered that the Transition Theory is complementary. Rising import prices, especially for raw materials, reduced profits and thus *ex post* returns to capital. If indeed, the rate of return on DC capital began to decline in the late 1960s this would provide an additional incentive for DC capital to relocate in the LDCs.

Another and no doubt related question is why it was that world real interest rates, both short-term and long-term,

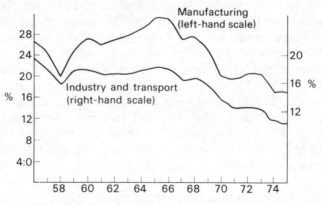

Source: Hill (1979)

Figure 4.16   *Pre-tax rates of return in developed countries 1956–75*

declined in the 1970s as Figure 4.17 shows. These data are *ex post* calculations, whereas what we really need to know are the expected real interest rates which must be calculated *ex ante*. Most probably the *ex post* decline in real interest rates during 1974–5 was not anticipated, since the OPEC oil price hikes took the world by surprise. But even if we ignore these years, Figure 4.17 suggests that real interest rates dropped by about two percentage points. One theory for the decline mentioned by Sachs (1981) is that OPEC's high savings ratio increased the supply of world savings following the redistribution of world income in favour of OPEC. Another theory is that the fall in capital returns in DCs was autonomous, reducing the demand for world capital and thus lowering the equilibrium real rate of interest. These are interesting issues, but since they lie beyond the purview of the Transition Theory we shall resist the temptation of considering them any further here.

The data in Figure 4.16 should not be taken for granted, since the measurement of capital returns is fraught with methodological difficulty. A sustained fall in the rate of return on capital is likely to depress share prices once it is anticipated by investors. Figure 4.18 plots world real share prices over the period 1966–80. Although a longer run of data would have been desirable, the chart does not indicate

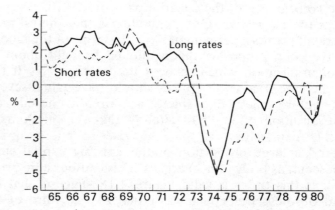

Source: London Business School, Centre for Economic Forecasting (unpublished data)

Figure 4.17   *Real interest rates in industrialised countries 1965–80*

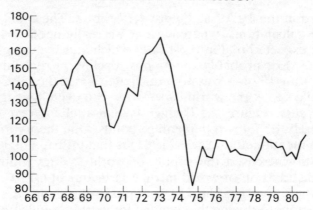

Source: London Business School, Centre for Economic Forecasting (unpublished data)

Figure 4.18   *Real world equity prices 1966–80 (1975 = 100)*

any weakening of share prices either in the late 1960s or in the early 1970s. Instead, the main feature of the chart is the collapse of real share prices after 1973 and the absence of any subsequent recovery. The collapse is all the more surprising since real share prices should move inversely with real interest rates. Since real interest rates fell real share prices should have risen.

The coincidence of the collapse with the OPEC oil price hikes is too suggestive. One possibility is that the oil price hikes dealt profits a permanent blow. In terms of the models we have been proposing this would be brought about by de-industrialisation which reduces the profit share. If this were the case, real equity prices should have fallen several years before they did since, as already noted, de-industrialisation effects had already taken root. A more plausible explanation is that the rise in energy prices rendered a large proportion of the existing capital stock obsolescent, as Baily (1981) argues. This caused share prices to fall. If this thesis is valid Figure 4.18 suggests that the capital obsolescence effect was equal to one third of the initial capital stock. It also suggests that post-1974 measures of capacity utilisation vastly understate the level of capacity utilisation.

(3) INTERNATIONAL CAPITAL FLOWS

We now turn to that aspect of the Transition Theory concerned with capital outflows from DCs to LDCs. Figure 4.19 plots capital flows into oil-importing developing countries (UN definition) at constant prices over the period 1960–80. It shows that during the early 1960s the inflow was stationary at approximately $10 billions per year, which is in line with the experience of the 1950s. During the second half of the 1960s the inflow begins to rise, so that even before the oil price hikes of 1973–4 it is clear that a structural break had occurred: LDC capital inflows in real terms had doubled in the space of five years. Therefore LDC borrowing on world capital markets was firmly established well before the OPEC oil price explosion. The LDC debt 'problem' existed before 1974. Figure 4.19 shows that since 1974 capital inflows have increased to an average inflow of about $28 billions, an increase of 40 per cent over its 1973 level. No doubt the peak inflows of 1974–5 and 1979–80 reflect the OPEC oil price rises that occurred in 1973–4 and 1978/9

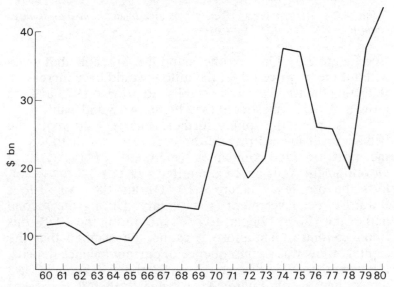

Source: *Compendium of World Development Indicators* (New York: UN) 1979 (updated to 1980)

Figure 4.19   *Capital flows to oil importing developing countries 1960–80 (at 1975 prices)*

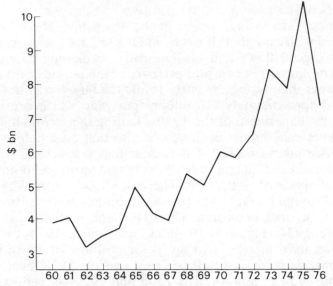

Source: Billerbeck and Yasugi (1979) Table S1.3, deflated by GDP deflator for market economies

Figure 4.20   *LDC inward private direct investment from industrialised countries 1960–76 (at 1975 prices)*

(see Figure 2.5). On the other hand it is arguable that, even without the oil price hikes, the inflow would have increased, reflecting the trend already established prior to 1973 and the growth of LDC investment (see Figure 4.15 and Table 4.2).

To establish this point further, Figure 4.20 plots the behaviour of inward private direct investment in LDCs on the part of DC companies (members of the OECD Development Assistance Committee – DAC). It broadly follows the profile of Figure 4.19. During the early 1960s inward direct investment is stationary. During the second half of the 1960s it begins to rise, and during the 1970s this trend continues. Therefore it cannot be claimed that the capital inflow was a consequence of current balance deficits. If it were there would be no reason for the increase in inward direct investment. Figure 4.20 suggests that there was a spontaneous increase in the flow of capital to LDCs on the part of DC companies. Because of the complementarity between private and social investment in the development process, LDC governments increased their international borrowing to finance infrastructure, urbanisation programmes, etc., which are all essential features of economic progress and industrialisation. It is simply wrong to regard such social investments as consumption by another name. The structural improvement in the LDC capital account position forced a structural deficit on the current account. This deficit largely reflected imports of capital goods (see Table 3.7) necessary for industrial development and which were financed by capital inflows.

Thus LDC indebtedness is not simply a disequilibrium consequence of the behaviour of world oil prices which threatens the international monetary system. It is an equilibrium or structural consequence of LDC industrialisation. As such it should not be a cause for concern. Indeed, attempts to frustrate this process in the mistaken interest of world monetary stability will undermine the legitimate spread of world development.

If this aspect of the Transition Theory is valid it should be reflected in the interest-rate structure of LDC borrowers on world capital markets. Countries that are running current balance deficits but are financing investment and industrialisation should enjoy lower borrowing costs. Countries that are running current balance deficits to finance consumption are likely to face higher borrowing costs. Below we report some econometric results obtained by Sachs (1981) based on a cross-section of thirty developing countries in 1979. The hypothesis he tested was that the premium (P) over LIBOR (London Interbank Offer Rate) should vary inversely with the ratio of investment to GNP (I/GNP) and directly with the current account deficit expressed as a proportion of GNP (CAD/GNP). He also assumed that richer LDCs would get better rates where wealth is measured by per capita GNP (GNP/POP) while higher debt ratios to GNP (D/GNP) would tend to increase the premium. These were his findings ('t' values are shown in parentheses):

$$P = 1.38 - 1.89 \text{ (I/GNP)} + 3.17 \text{ (CAD/GNP)}$$
$$(5.7) \quad (2.2) \qquad\qquad (3.2)$$
$$- 0.009 \text{ (GNP/POP)} + 0.0008 \text{ (D/GNP)}$$
$$(1.4) \qquad\qquad\qquad (0.2)$$

$$\bar{R}^2 = 0.35 \qquad \text{standard error} = 0.26$$

The equation confirms that the higher the investment ratio the lower the premium. Investment ratios range from zero up to 50 per cent. The equation therefore implies that this will contribute to a range of premiums of about one percentage point relative to LIBOR. The equation also implies that if an increase in investment is wholly supported by imports the premium will rise since the coefficient of CAD/GNP is greater than the coefficient of I/GNP. These results tend to confirm the hypothesis that capital markets recognise that borrowing for investment is legitimate and this lends support to the Transition Theory.

Not surprisingly, Table 4.3 shows that the manufacturing sector has taken the lion's share of private inward direct investment in developing countries. Recalling that manufactures in 1970 accounted for 18 per cent of LDC GDP, manufactures' share of increased direct investment is disproportionately large. This reflects DC investors' perception that world comparative advantage has shifted in favour of LDCs as far as manufactures are concerned. Moreover, if we ignore the petroleum sector (which is something of a special case), Table 4.4 shows that over the period 1965–72 manufactures' share of inward direct investment has tended to rise.

Finally, we note that in real terms global LDC indebtedness has not grown very much, thanks to inflation. Figure 4.21 shows that since 1972 nominal indebtedness has about quadrupled. However, real indebtedness has increased by only 50 per cent. In these calculations the LDC export price deflator is used. This implies that inflation has transferred resources from DCs to LDCs, since debtors gain and cred-

Table 4.3 *Sectoral shares of private investment flows to developing countries 1965–72 (average annual flows)*

	$ Millions	% of total
Petroleum	1027	33.3
Mining and smelting	233	7.6
Manufacturing	1148	37.2
Other	674	21.4
TOTAL	3082	100.0

Source: Billerbeck and Yasugi (1979) Table II.3

Table 4.4 *Manufactures' share of inward direct investment in developing countries 1965–72 (%)*

1965–66	53.8
1967–68	53.0
1969–70	62.3
1971–72	55.0

Source: Billerbeck and Yasugi (1979) Table SI.6

itors lose because of inflation. Elementary inflation accounting implies that this transfer averaged $10 billion per year at 1972 prices over the period 1973–80, which compares with official development assistance which averaged $8.5 billion over a similar period. In other words, inflation was more important for transferring resources to LDCs than aid. Figure 4.21 plots the time distribution of this transfer and shows that it was most pronounced during the earlier and latter parts of the 1970s.

For similar reasons, the debt service indicators shown on Figure 4.22 do not show any dramatic changes over the

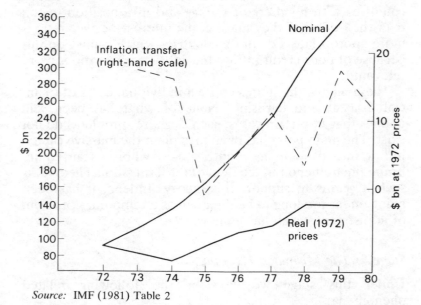

Source: IMF (1981) Table 2

Figure 4.21 *Medium- and long-term debt of 94 developing countries 1972–9*

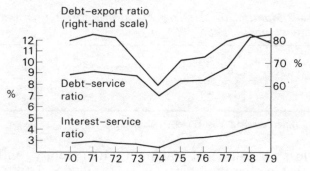

Source: World Bank (1981) p. 58

Figure 4.22   *Developing country debt ratios 1970–9*

1970s. The debt–service ratio is defined as interest plus payments of principal on long-term debt, divided by exports of goods and services. The interest–service ratio excludes repayments of principal. The debt–exports ratio is self-explanatory. The former ratios rose slightly towards the end of the decade. The latter ratio has remained stable over the decade. None of the ratios indicates cause for concern. For countries with good credit ratings and in a position to roll over their debts as they mature, the interest–service ratio is more appropriate. For those countries which cannot do this because of poor credit ratings the debt–service ratio is more relevant.

These aggregate figures conceal individual cases of financial disaster and hardship. None of what has been said implies that in certain cases, such as Zaire, problems do not exist. The main point has been to explain the massive capital inflow into developing countries as a whole as an equilibrium phenomenon in the light of the Transition Theory. As such it seems to support this theory. Indeed, it has been going on far too long to be regarded as a temporary problem of adjustment which has gone wrong.

Stage 5: The Mismatch Hypothesis

Under this stage we consider the following related phenomena:

- the rise in unemployment in the industrialised countries,

and
- the sectoral distribution of unemployment and excess capacity.

It will be recalled that the insight of the mismatch theory is that, as resources are forced to move from one sector of the economy to another, excess supply conditions build up in the manufacturing sector while excess demand conditions and bottlenecks are manifest in the rest of the economy. During this transition, unemployment as a whole tends to increase. We thus have an explanation of the paradox of shortage amidst unemployment. Typically, the service sectors in the 1970s have been booming while the manufacturing sector has been recessed. There is an underlying dualism to the recession in the West, just as there is an underlying dualism to world economic developments. The world recession has bypassed the LDCs. The DC recession has largely bypassed the non-manufacturing sector and has only affected manufacturing. It should be clear by now that according to the Transition Theory these dualisms are related.

The Transition Theory is complementary to other theories of unemployment, so that unemployment is caused by other factors, which might affect other sectors of the DC economy apart from manufactures. Three main complementary theories may be cited:

(1) *Raw materials and unemployment:* in Chapter 2 it was argued that an increase in imported raw materials prices reduces equilibrium real wage rates. If labour markets do not adjust instantaneously, classical unemployment will be generated because the supply price of labour is greater than the demand price. This unemployment will persist until real wages fall to their new equilibrium level. The revolution in raw materials prices in the late 1960s and the OPEC oil price hikes may have generated classical unemployment of this type.

(2) *Keynesian unemployment:* in Keynesian models of the economy falls in the level of aggregate demand brought about by negative real balance or wealth effects, contractions of world trade, government expenditure, etc.,

will reduce employment and increase the level of un-employment. Thus an increase in commodity prices or the price of oil induces world recession, either because it reduces the level of disposable income or because it reduces the volume of real money balances or wealth. In most Keynesian models these effects are temporary, since aggregate demand eventually reverts to its under-lying 'natural' level. Thus classical unemployment occurs when relative prices are wrong. In contrast, Keynesian unemployment rises when the absolute price level is too high. This distinction has been discus-sed at length by Malinvaud (1977).

(3) *New classical unemployment:* according to the so-called 'new classical' theory, see e.g. Beenstock (1980), un-employment only rises when expectations are not ful-filled and when agents are taken by surprise by economic events. Thus in so far as people did not anti-cipate the increase in commodity or oil prices un-employment will be generated. If instead they correctly anticipated such events, wages and prices will have adjusted in advance so that when the events themselves actually occur the economy is fully braced to meet them.

A full analysis of OECD unemployment is beyond our present mandate and all of the above theories no doubt form part of the story. Our present objective is the less ambitious one of examining unemployment data to see if it provides *prima facie* support for the Transition Theory and the mis-match hypothesis. With this in mind, Figure 4.23 plots the history of DC unemployment over the period 1954–80. The index is a weighted average of the unemployment rates of the principal OECD countries. The index shows that DC unemployment fell until 1966. During the second half of the 1960s this trend was reversed and unemployment began to rise. During the 1970s it rose sharply and the chart strongly suggests that the OPEC oil price hikes of 1973–4 contri-buted to the subsequent growth of unemployment.

Given our present concerns, the most important feature of the chart is that a structural break in the behaviour of DC unemployment occurred well before the OPEC oil price

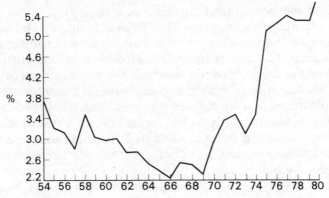

Source: *Labour Statistics* (Paris: OECD) various issues

Figure 4.23 *Unemployment rates of the civilian labour force in developed countries 1954–80*

hikes and well before the resurgence of inflation in the early 1970s. Indeed, the seeds of the unemployment problem of the 1970s were sown in the second half of the 1960s. This timing and the direction of the structural break coincide with the predictions of the Transition Theory. There are no theories (to my knowledge) which explain why it was that after a secular tendency to decline unemployment began to grow from 1967. By 1972, i.e. before the OPEC price hikes, unemployment had returned to a level last seen in the early 1950s. Thus within the space of six years the unemployment clock had been turned back twenty years.

The oil price disturbances from 1973 onwards make it difficult to unscramble the various theoretical effects noted above. This is a shame, because LDC industrialisation continued unabated during the 1970s and it would have been desirable to monitor the Transition Theory over this long period. But we must be grateful for small mercies, and the period up to 1973 provides at least some empirical basis for assessing the Transition Theory.

The evidence in Figure 4.23 only provides indirect confirmation for the mismatch hypothesis. To find direct evidence it would be necessary to compare excess supply conditions in the manufacturing sector with market conditions elsewhere in the economy. This presents formidable

data and methodological difficulties, although perhaps the
popular perception supports the mismatch thesis. The very
fact that de-industrialisation is a word invented during the
1970s seems to support this view. However, we cannot rely
solely on the folklore of the times. If the mismatch theory is
valid, manufacturing unemployment should rise relative to
unemployment as a whole. As was argued in Chapter 3, this
increase should last only as long as it takes the mismatch in
the economy to sort itself out. Therefore we should expect a
temporary if protracted increase in the share of manufacturing unemployment.

Unfortunately, global data are not available on this. Nor is
it easy to construct an appropriate index. Nevertheless, Figure 4.24 plots these ratios for the UK, the US and Canada.
The contribution of the manufacturing sector to unemployment is cyclical and varies directly with unemployment as a whole (compare Figures 4.23 and 4.24).
During the first half of the 1960s the share of manufacturing
unemployment was declining. Between 1959 and 1966 the
share fell from 28 per cent to 22 per cent in the US, and in
the UK it fell from 33 per cent to 27 per cent. In Canada this
development was less pronounced.

According to the Transition Theory, mismatch unemployment and thus the share of manufacturing un-

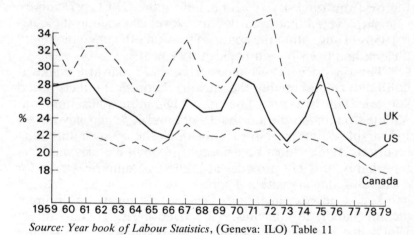

Source: Year book of Labour Statistics, (Geneva: ILO) Table 11

Figure 4.24 Shares of manufacturing unemployment in total
unemployment 1959–79 (%)

employment should rise during the second half of the 1960s. Figure 4.24 suggests that this occurred in the US over the period 1966–75 and that it occurred in the UK over the period 1965–72. This also occurred to some extent in Canada over the same period. These admittedly crude measures indicate the presence of mismatch effects, but they do not seem to be protracted and last no more than a decade at the outside.

There is something decidedly odd about the data recorded on Figure 4.24. According to Figure 4.24, the ratio of manufacturing unemployment to total UK unemployment fell during the 1970s. Yet Figure 8.7 indicates that manufacturing employment fell not only in relative terms, but also in absolute terms. It is therefore difficult to believe that the dole queue in the manufacturing sector failed to grow relative to the dole queue for the economy as a whole. Perhaps the problem lies in the fact that, while we can identify the sectoral origins of the unemployed, we cannot meaningfully classify them in terms of manufacturing unemployed or non-manufacturing employed.

Mismatch effects may occur in the capital markets in addition to and independently from their manifestation in labour markets. Just as labour is unlikely to migrate effortlessly from declining to expanding sectors of the economy, so capital is unlikely to relocate without friction. This is especially the case if capital is putty-clay and the costs of redeploying capital in the expanding sectors are large. Unfortunately there is no direct evidence on mismatch in the market for physical capital. If, however, capital in the manufacturing sector is less productive because of mismatch effects, the market valuation of this capital will fall relative to the market valuation of capital elsewhere in the economy. Figure 4.25 plots the ratio of the *Financial Times* Actuaries Share Index for 'capital goods' to the 'all-share' index of UK securities. While it is not ideal, the former index corresponds reasonably well to an index of manufacturing, although it excludes textiles and food manufacturing. On the other hand, it does include motors, electricals, engineering and metals. The chart indicates that during the first half of the 1960s the capital goods sector was performing relatively well. However, between 1965 and 1975 there was a dramatic decline in relative share valuations which is suggestive

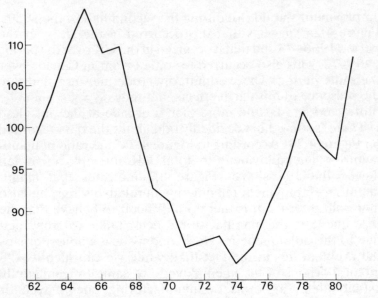

Source: London Business School Share Price Data Base

Figure 4.25   *Relative share price of UK capital goods industries 1962–81 (1968 = 100)*

of a mismatch effect of a pronounced kind. More recently, despite the dramatic fall in manufacturing output since 1979 relative share valuations have improved and in January 1982 the index had returned to its level of seventeen years before.

II   Formal data analysis

Methodology

In this section we explore some econometric relationships that bear upon the Transition Theory. This is not a genuine modelling exercise in the sense that it is not our intention to develop a working model of the world economy. Rather it complements the informal empirical analysis in the previous section. It may be that the data we use do not match the high-powered nature of modern statistical techniques. Others might argue that these techniques are not sophisti-cated enough to make a full evaluation of the Transition

Theory and that they lend themselves to spurious accuracy. Perhaps the most that can be achieved at the present time is what has already been done in Part I, i.e. to look at the data and to see if their timing and qualitative changes conflict or conform with the Transition Theory.

The results that are reported should be regarded as 'interpretive search' in the sense described by Leamer (1978). We simply wish to see if the data can be interpreted in the light of the Transition Theory. This does not, of course, rule out the importance of other theories either as complements or substitutes. Since the relationships that are explored are unlikely to be valid at every moment in time and instead are proposed as long-run equilibrium propositions, it is necessary to use econometric techniques that allow for divergencies between short- and long-run economic behaviour. Following Davidson *et al.* (1978) the so-called 'error correction' methodology is applied in which short-term economic behaviour reflects temporary shocks, adjustments towards the long run equilibrium and changes in the long run equilibrium itself.

Let us assume for purposes of illustration that the long run relationship between two variables, Y and X, is

$$\ln Y = \alpha_0 + \alpha_1 \ln X$$

At any moment in time this relationship may not hold because random disturbances (u) have cause Y to deviate from its equilibrium, or because a variable Z has a temporary influence on Y, or because X has changed and Y cannot adjust to X instantaneously. Denoting time subscripts by t-i, we may thus dynamise the equilibrium relationship between Y and X as

$$\Delta \ln Y_t = \beta_0 + \beta_1 \Delta \ln Z_t + \beta_2 \Delta \ln X_t -$$
$$\beta_3 \ln(Y/X)_{t-1} + \beta_4 \ln X_{t-1} + u_t$$

where {u} is white noise. The stationary state of this equation is obtained by setting terms in Δ to zero:

$$\ln Y = \frac{\beta_0}{\beta_3} + \frac{(\beta_3 + \beta_4)}{\beta_3} \ln X$$

i.e.

$$\alpha_0 = \frac{\beta_0}{\beta_3} \qquad \alpha_1 = \frac{\beta_3 + \beta_4}{\beta_3}$$

Therefore Z affects Y in the short term but not in the long term, since it does not appear in the stationary state. X affects Y in the short and long terms according to the lag distribution implied by β_2, β_3 and β_4. Clearly, more complicated 'error correction' models may be conceived with more sophisticated lag distributions. In every case below, the error correction models and their associated stationary states are reported. The observation period is 1950–78 and the observations are annual.

Relative Prices

We begin by investigating the relationship between the relative price index (PCOM), plotted on Figure 4.3, and LDC industrialisation. The basic thesis is that as LDC industrial production (IP_{LDC}) rises, the price of commodities rises relative to the price of manufactures. However, previous research e.g. Panic and Enoch (1981), suggests that the level of economic activity in developed countries (GDP_{DC}) will exert upward pressure on relative commodity prices. Therefore the model is

$$PCOM = F(\overset{+}{IP}_{LDC}, \overset{+}{GDP}_{DC}, t)$$

where t is a time trend and the signs of partial derivatives are shown above the variables to which they refer. To capture the influence of GDP_{DC} and LDC industrial production on real commodity prices a model of the form was fitted (standard errors in parentheses)

$$\Delta \ln PCOM_t = -4.07 - 0.604\ \Delta\ln PCOM_{t-1}$$
$$(2.29)\ \ (0.156)$$
$$- 1.08\ \Delta\ln PCOM_{t-2} - 0.731\ \ln PCOM_{t-3}$$
$$(0.157) \qquad\qquad (0.22)$$
$$+ 0.916\ \ln GDP_{DCt} + 1.303\ \Delta_4 \ln GDP_{DCt}$$
$$(0.63) \qquad\qquad (0.68)$$
$$+ 0.01\ IP_{LDCt} - 0.089\ t$$
$$(0.0025) \qquad (0.03)$$
$$\bar{R}^2 = 0.71 \qquad \sigma = 0.058 \qquad LM(7.81) = 4.77$$

which has the stationary state solution

$$\ln \text{PCOM} = 1.25 \ln\text{GDP}_{DC} + 0.14 \text{ IP}_{LDC} - 0.122 \text{ t}$$

LM(N) is a lagrange multiplier test for the randomness of the residual autocorrelogram. It has a χ^2 distribution and N is the critical value at $p = 0.05$. Therefore in the above equation the estimated correlogram is random. The test is especially suited to equations containing lagged endogenous variable. Further details are given in Godfrey (1978).

This equation confirms the oscillatory behaviour of real commodity prices and shows that output shocks in the DCs exert important short run and long run influences on commodity prices. The equation further shows that industrial expansion in the LDCs has the effect of lowering manufactured prices relative to commodity prices. We interpret this as a supply shock in the sense that higher manufacturing supply reduces the relative price of manufactures on the world market. Notice it is not $\ln\text{IP}_{LDC}$ that has been specified but IP_{LDC}. The semi-logarithmic specification implies that the elasticity of PCOM with respect to IP_{LDC} is equal to 0.0141 IP_{LDC}, i.e. it rises with IP_{LDC} itself. This is to allow for the growing importance of LDC industrial production in the world economy. It implies that a 10 per cent increase in LDC industrial production causes the relative price of manufactures to fall by about 15 per cent.

De-industrialisation

The next step is to trace the relationship between these relative prices and the share of industrial production in DC GDP. The Transition Theory implies that the industrial production ratio varies inversely with PCOM. In addition, however, we assume that this ratio also depends on engle curve effects. Our specification is

$$\text{IP/GDP} = F(\overset{-}{\text{PCOM}}, \overset{+/-}{\text{GDP}}, t)$$

The indeterminate sign reflects the indeterminacy of the engle curve effects. If industrial production is an inferior good, $\partial F/\partial GDP$ is negative. The negative effect of PCOM is also consistent with the model described in Chapter 2, where it was shown that higher imported raw materials prices might induce de-industrialisation.

Using the data already described the fitted error correction model was:

$$\Delta \ln(IP/GDP)_t = -8.6 - 1.1 \, \Delta \ln(IP/GDP)_{t-1}$$
$$(1.66)(0.12)$$
$$- 1.53 \, \Delta \ln(IP/GDP)_{t-2}$$
$$(0.26)$$
$$- 1.75 \, \ln(IP/GDP)_{t-3} - 0.05 \, \ln PCOM_{t-1}$$
$$(0.33) \qquad\qquad (0.025)$$
$$+ 0.79 \, \ln GDP_t + 0.46 \, \ln GDP_{t-2}$$
$$(0.11) \qquad\qquad (0.26)$$
$$- 0.045t$$
$$(0.0088)$$

$$\bar{R}^2 = 0.83 \qquad \sigma = 0.011 \qquad LM(7.81) = 1.45$$

The stationary state solution to this model is

$$\ln(IP/GDP) = -0.0286 \, \ln PCOM$$
$$+ 0.714 \, \ln GDP - 0.0257 \, t$$

Thus the de-industrialisation hypothesis is supported, although the absolute effect is small. On the other hand, the engle curve effect is positive although the large negative time trend might be correlated with the high coefficient on GDP. It is also possible that the positive engle curve effect reflects cyclical rather than secular phenomena, i.e. industrial production tends to be more cyclically variable. The equation implies that an autonomous increase of LDC industrial production of 10 per cent reduces the industrial production ratio in DCs by about one and a half percentage points, i.e. recalling that PCOM rises by 15 per cent and the initial value of the ratio was approximately 30 per cent.

Further corroboration of the Transition Theory comes from an econometric analysis of the DC profit share (see Figure 4.11). The hypothesis is that as PCOM rises the profit share falls, because of the profit share (Π) and the industrial production ratio move in the same direction, under the plausible assumption that industrial output is relatively capital intensive. In addition, however, the price of energy may affect the factorial distribution of income. Below, the real price of energy is assumed to be related to the real price of OPEC oil (PEN) shown in Figure 2.3. Hence our basic specification is

$$\Pi = F(\text{PC}\bar{\text{O}}\text{M}, \overset{?}{\text{PEN}}, t)$$

The effect of energy prices is indeterminate in theory but it might be thought that higher energy prices would affect profits rather than wages, at least in the first instance. Indeed if, as Berndt and Wood (1979) claim, the aggregate production function is weakly separable with respect to labour, i.e.

$$Q = F(L, G(K, E))$$

then a rise in real energy prices which brings about a fall in energy usage (E) causes the return on capital to fall while real wage rates are unchanged. This implies that $\partial F/\partial \text{PEN} < 0$, assuming K and L are unchanged. If, in addition, K/L falls because the return on capital has fallen below its cost, the profit share will be drawn down for this reason too.

The results below do not confirm the Berndt–Wood thesis, since $\partial F/\partial \text{PEN} < 0$, i.e. the labour market is more adversely affected than the capital market when energy prices rise. Since, however, the observation period ended in 1975, it is possible that the effect of the OPEC price hikes on the profit share had not yet materialised and it is quite possible that a longer observation period would produce a different result.

The fitted error correction model was

$$\ln\Pi_t = 0.329 + 0.855 \ln\Pi_{t-1} - 0.156 \ln\text{PCOM}_{t-1}$$
$$\quad (0.276) \quad (0.088) \qquad\quad (0.061)$$
$$\quad + 0.0623 \ln\text{PEN}_{t-1}$$
$$\quad\quad (0.021)$$

$$\bar{R}^2 = 0.912 \qquad \sigma = 0.024 \qquad \text{LM}(7.81) = 4.75$$

which has the following stationary state solution

$$\ln\Pi = -1.36\ \ln\text{PCOM} + 0.54\ \ln\text{PEN}$$

The equation implies that an autonomous 10 per cent increase in LDC industrial production which causes relative commodity prices to rise by 15 per cent and the DC industrial production ratio to fall by about one and a half percentage points, causes the profit share to fall by about six percentage points from an initial level of 30 per cent. This decline approximately equals the actual fall in the profit share over the decade up to 1975 (see Figure 4.11).

Mismatch Hypothesis

The central insight of the mismatch thesis is that the effect of LDC industrialisation on GDP in the developed countries is adverse, but only temporarily so. Because of the mismatch of supply and demand in the DC economy there is not an immediate change in the allocation of resources. Indeed the equation for the industrial production ratio bears this out, since a non-trivial distributed lag relationship was found to exist between relative prices and the industrial production ratio. In terms of 'error correction' methodology LDC industrialisation (measured by the change in LDC GDP) is classified as a Z variable, i.e. it has a temporary influence on the dynamics of the model but does not effect the stationary state. In terms of Figure 3.7 the economy temporarily moves inside the production possibility frontier before the new equilibrium allocation of resources is achieved.

To explore the mismatch thesis it is assumed that the long run level of GDP in the DCs is supply-determined and therefore depends on the supply of factors of production. In the short run, however, the level of output may be depressed by mismatch effects as well as cyclical phenemena. In the model below the latter are represented by changes in real money balances (M/P). Therefore, the stationary-state specification for GDP in the DCs is

$$\text{GDP}^*_{\text{DC}} = F(\overset{+}{K}, \overset{+}{L}, \overset{+}{E}, t)$$

and the short term specification is

$$\Delta GDP_{DC} = G(\Delta G\bar{D}P_{LDC}, \Delta \overset{+}{M}/P, \Delta G\overset{+}{D}P^{*}_{DC}, G\bar{D}P_{DC}/GDP^{*}_{DC})$$

which also implies that real money balances are also Z variables because they do not affect the stationary-state value of GDP in the developed countries.

In the estimated error correction model it was impossible to integrate all of these variables. The main problem arose with the level of employment which failed to be significant, perhaps because it is colinear with the other factor of production. Therefore in the equation below L is omitted. The fitted model is

$$\Delta \ln GDP_{DCt} = -1.91 + 2.43\ \Delta \ln K_t + 0.381\ \ln K_{t-2}$$
$$\quad (0.53)\ \ (1.2) \qquad\qquad (0.12)$$
$$+ 0.413\ \Delta \ln E_t - 0.613\ \ln GDP_{DCt-1}$$
$$(0.12) \qquad\qquad (0.16)$$
$$+ 0.68\ \Delta \ln(M/P)_t - 0.0033\ \Delta GDP_{LDCt-1}$$
$$(0.07) \qquad\qquad (0.0016)$$
$$+ 0.167\ \ln E_{t-1}$$
$$(0.11)$$

$$\bar{R}^2 = 0.75 \qquad \sigma = 0.01 \qquad LM(7.81) = 5.53$$

and the stationary state solution is

$$\ln GDP_{DC} = 0.62\ \ln K + 0.27\ \ln E$$

The coefficient on $\Delta \ln GDP_{LDC}$ is negative, as the mismatch theory implies, and it is statistically significant. It implies that if there is an autonomous expansion in LDC GDP of 10 per cent, GDP in developed countries falls, but by only 0.033 per cent. In addition, it implies that the period of mismatch is not very long; 85 per cent of the disequilibrium is eradicated after two years of adjustment. Therefore while these results confirm the qualitative deductions of the mismatch thesis their quantitative importance does not appear to be very great. At this stage, however, we are more concerned with quality rather than quantity. In Chapter 6 other evidence is brought to bear on the latter aspects. Finally, the equation implies that a real balance expansion of 1 per cent raises the level of output by 0.68 per cent in the short term, but has no long-term effect.

Energy

In the last equation the level of energy consumption (E) is assumed to be given. Using a similar econometric methodology, Beenstock and Willcocks (1981) estimate an energy demand function for developed market economies which is assumed to vary directly with the level of economic activity (GDP) and inversely with the real price of OPEC oil. The stationary state of the commercial demand equation is

$$\ln E = 1.546 \, \ln GDP_{DC} - 0.0264 \, \ln PEN + 0.0257t$$

Combining this result with the stationary-state equation for GDP_{DC}, and assuming that the capital stock remains unchanged, implies that the elasticity of GDP_{DC} with respect to PEN is -0.0071. This in turn implies that a quadrupling of the real price of oil reduces the level of output in developed countries by about 1.7 per cent. This effect is permanent and should not be confused with the temporary recession effect of the fall in real money balances which higher oil prices bring in their wake, especially when governments lean into the inflationary wind. These effects are discussed at length in Chapter 7.

5

The Long Wave Hypothesis

Kondratieff

This chapter considers the possibility that the deceleration of growth among the industrialised countries since the late 1960s reflects long-term cycles in economic activity that were first identified by Kondratieff (1935). The Kondratieff cycle is spread over roughly half a century and consists of twenty-five years of boom followed by twenty-five years of slump. In the present context the boom years would consist of the 1940s and 1950s and most of the 1960s. If, in fact, an autonomous Kondratieff cycle exists, it may be that the slump of the 1970s reflects the unravelling of Kondratieff forces. If so, the last two decades or so of the twentieth century are likely to be years of slump and stagnation. It is worth pointing out that Kondratieff first carried out his research in the early 1920s, i.e. before the onset of the interwar depression, and his data period finished in 1920. He identified 1920 as the peak of the upswing, implying that approximately twenty-five years of depression lay ahead. He was not far wrong.

Renewed interest in Kondratieff largely reflects the efforts of Rostow (1978, 1980), who argues that the recession of the 1970s is to be understood in terms of long-term economic forces of this type. Kondratieff himself did not offer a theory to explain his cycles although he proposed a number of *ad hoc* suggestions which Rostow and others later drew on.

● Changes in technique: the rhythm of economic life may

reflect the rhythm of invention and scientific discovery. However, he suggested that the latter may not necessarily be autonomous and instead may be induced by economic forces.

- War and revolutions: these may induce cycles but may also reflect economic developments.
- Colonisation: the opening up of new lands may induce cycles but he argued that it was more probable that colonisation was endogenously determined.
- Gold production: discovery of new mines and techniques of gold production may induce cycles. However, Kondratieff persuaded himself that this factor, too, is probably induced and not external to the system.

In contrast Rostow, Schumpeter (1934) and Kuznets have developed formal theories of long-term cyclical fluctuations. However, Kuznets (1961) identified twenty-year cycles in US economic behaviour which reflected cycles of immigration and building activity. These cycles are too short, given our present interests, and in any case were specifically related to waves of US immigration which, as Abramovitz (1964) has pointed out, have come to an end. Therefore we shall ignore the Kuznets cycle and concentrate instead on Rostow and Schumpeter. Likewise we ignore other cycles such as Kitchen (3 years) and Juglar (9 years). Our main conclusion is that the Rostovian and Schumpetrian theories are unhelpful in the present context. It may be possible *ex post* to explain economic cycles, but this does not mean that they are of any, *ex ante* importance. More generally, we argue that there are no iron laws of economic rise and decline.There are no economic forces that mean economies must experience relatively long periods of boom followed by relatively long periods of slump. This leads us to rule out the theory that OECD countries are inevitably caught up in a Kondratieff slump.

It should be emphasised that Kondratieff never studied the level of economic activity (GDP or industrial production) because these data were not available to him, although he did study production data for coal, lead and pig iron over a shorter time horizon. Instead his main data source consisted of commodity prices in France, the US and England over the period 1780–1920. Figure 5.1 shows his original data. Kondratieff concluded from this data that there were two and a half long waves, as summarised in Table 5.1. The first thing to note is that these cycles are not very obvious to the naked eye, and it certainly cannot be a foregone conclusion that these systematic waves do in fact exist. Secondly, the relationship between price movements and economic activity is not transparent. Kondratieff himself does not amplify this relationship although he recognises (p. 108) that his 'study however, would lose much of its force if we did not also analyse the behaviour of purely physical series'. Subsequent interpretations have been based on the premise that price upswings are brought about by booms and downswings by slumps.

Since the data in Figure 5.1 do not reveal obvious cycles, some more comprehensive statistical tests were carried out. Using the precise data that Kondratieff himself used, the spectral density functions of the US and English price series were estimated. Kondratieff had 132 annual observations on US wholesale price data and 143 observations on English wholesale prices. We have therefore not supplemented this data with observations beyond 1920. This was because we

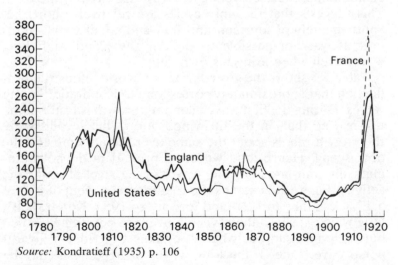

Source: Kondratieff (1935) p. 106

Figure 5.1 *The Kondratieff price wave (index numbers for commodity prices, 1901–10 = 100)*

Table 5.1 *Kondratieff's long waves*

Wave	Upswing	Downswing
1	1780–90 to 1810–17	1810–17 to 1844–51
2	1844–51 to 1870–75	1870–75 to 1890–96
3	1890–96 to 1914–20	

Source: Kondratieff (1935)

wanted to check whether the Kondratieff cycle was implied by Kondratieff's own evidence.

It is, of course, extremely hazardous to infer fifty-year cycles from relatively short data sets and spectral estimation would require at least 400 observations. Nevertheless Figure 5.2 plots the logarithms of the spectral density functions using a Parzen window with a truncation point of eighty observations. The peaks of the spectral density functions imply cycle lengths as indicated on Table 5.2. Most probably only those asterisked are significant. Thus the long eighty- and twenty-year cycles are most probably not significant because the respective peaks in the spectral density function are not well-defined. When the series were first differenced an additional fourteen-year cycle was suggested by the data. This suggests that the only cycles are relatively short, i.e. approximately of fourteen and four-and-a-half years' duration. It was not possible to discern any Kondratieff long waves even when using his own data.

Table 5.3 shows the growth rates of 'world' industrial production that approximately correspond to Kondratieff's long waves. During the first wave economic growth is faster in the downswing than in the upswing. During the second wave the growth rate is about the same over the upswing and the downswing. Hence long waves in price data do not automatically translate into long waves in the level of economic activity. Figure 5.3 extends the English component of Figure 5.1 back in time to 1264 and forward to 1954. Kondratieff's long waves are just about visible over the period he studied but seem to disappear when one takes a broader historical perspective. Indeed, the long waves of hypothesis may be submitted to more systematic tests as described below (pp. 145ff).

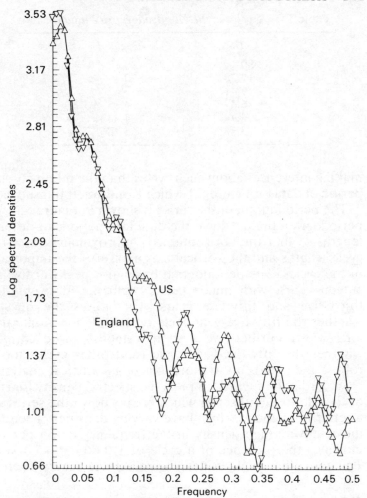

Figure 5.2 *Power spectrum of Kondratieff's wholesale price data for England and the US*

Lord Beveridge compiled annual data on European wheat prices over the period 1500–1869. While a more general price index would have been preferable, it is worth considering whether Beveridge's series displays long cycles as suggested by Kondratieff. More specifically, does the series indicate the presence of a fifty-year cycle? Close to four centuries of data should provide a more reliable basis for

Table 5.2   *Cycles in the Kondratieff price data (years)*

US	England
80	80
17.78	20
9.41	6.67
6.4	4.85
4.44*	4.44*
3.33	3.48*

making inferences about such cycles than the relatively short period of data on Figure 5.1 which Kondratieff himself used.

The periodogram of the series is shown in Figure 5.4. The periodogram breaks down the data into periods of different lengths so that the horizontal axis approximately measures cycle lengths and the vertical axis measures the importance of the cycles. The periodogram has major peaks at five and fifteen years, with minor peaks occurring at twenty-five, thirty-five and fifty-five years. This raises the question whether the fifty-five-year cycle represents the Kondratieff long wave. Further, we wish to establish more correctly whether the fifty-five-year cycle (and other cycles too) is robust and stands up to more exacting statistical analysis.

Accordingly, Figure 5.5 plots the spectral density function of the (de-trended) series which breaks down the series into a set of frequencies which have varying densities. Therefore the relatively high density at the frequency 0.065 per year indicates the presence of a cycle of $1/0.065 = 15.4$ years. The only other peak, if it can be called one occurs when the

Table 5.3   *Growth .in 'world' industrial production during Kondratieff's long wave periods (% per annum)*

Wave	Upswing	Downswing
1	1785–1820: 2.4	1820–1840: 2.9
2	1840–1870: 3.2	1870–1894: 3.2
3	1894–1913: 4.6	

Source: Rostow (1978) p. 622

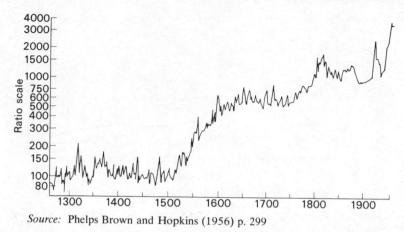

Source: Phelps Brown and Hopkins (1956) p. 299

Figure 5.3   *Price of a composite unit of consumables in southern England 1264–1954 (1451–75 = 100)*

frequency is 0.19, which would suggest the presence of a cycle of 5.25 years. These cycles are also reflected in the periodogram. However, the estimated power spectrum of the series rules out the presence of long cycles including the fifty-five-year cycle, suggesting that these cycles are no more than statistical artefacts. These results cast doubt on the statistical evidence for fifty-year price cycles.

Figure 5.6 plots the spectral density function of the price

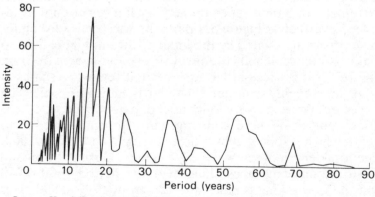

Source: Kendall and Stuart (1968) Vol. III, p. 459

Figure 5.4   *Periodogram of the Beveridge wheat price series 1500–1869*

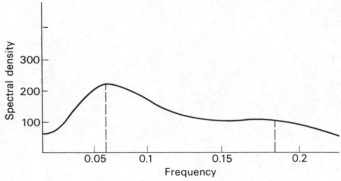

Source: Kendall and Stuart (1968) vol. III, p. 456

Figure 5.5   *Power   spectrum   of   the   Beveridge   wheat   price   series 1500–1869*

series shown in Figure 5.3. The time series has been first differenced to induce stationarity in the data and a Parzen window has been used with a fifty-period truncation point. The two main peaks occur when the frequencies are 0.04 and 0.16. These correspond to cycle lengths of 157 and forty years respectively. Other cycles occur at twenty-seven and fourteen years. It is possible that the fifty-year cycle is a close neighbour to Kondratieff's fifty-year cycle. Indeed Shirk (1975) claims that this series incorporates a number of cycles in the vicinity of fifty years.

As stated before, price movements are not necessarily related to the level of economic activity. Unfortunately, extremely long time series on activity indices are not available. Nevertheless Figure 5.7 plots the wage index for building craftsmen, deflated by the index shown in Figure 5.3. To make inferences about the level of economic activity from Figure 5.7 it is necessary to assume that real wage shares in GDP are roughly constant. The charts indicates some long waves but these are very long indeed, extending over two to three centuries. There is an upswing from about 1325 to 1450, which is followed by a downswing from 1450 to 1600. The total length of this wave is 275 years. During the second wave the upswing takes place over the period 1600–1740 and the downswing is much shorter, from 1740–1800. This gives rise to a wave of 200 years. The chart terminates with an upswing of about 150 years.

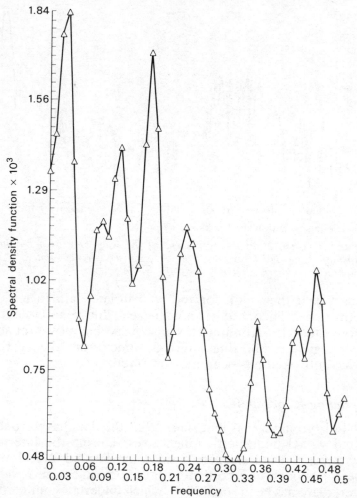

Figure 5.6 *Power spectrum of the southern English price data 1264–1954*

No attempt will be made here to explain these waves. Nor does the author claim credit for the discovery of the Beenstock Cycle. The moral of this story is that optical illusions may always exist with time series and, epistemologically speaking, the cart has been put before the horse. Despite the excitement of it, data should never be in search of a theory to 'explain' them. Instead we must begin with

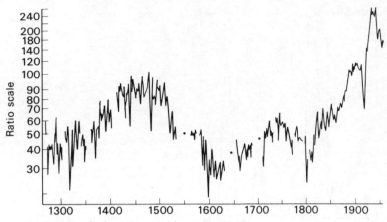

Source: Phelps Brown and Hopkins (1956) p. 302

Figure 5.7   *Changes in the equivalent of the wage rate of a building craftsman 1264–1954 (expressed in a composite physical unit of consumables in southern England; 1451–75 = 100)*

theory and then look for the appropriate data to test its deductions. Theory does not suggest 200-year cycles or fifty-year cycles. Kondratieff's 'discovery' has most probably been a great red herring, although some of the 'theory' that is has provoked has been most inspired.

Updating Kondratieff

The disturbing fact is that since 1920 the data have broadly fitted with Kondratieff's long waves. During the interwar years prices even stagnated; since the Second World War there has been unprecedented inflation. Since 1969, however, there has been stagflation, which underlines our earlier point that the relationship between prices and output is not transparent.

Table 5.4 draws on Madison's (1977) identification of phases of economic growth for advanced capitalist countries. It also draws on Kahn's (1979) classifications and florid descriptions. The first thing to note is that the upswings and downswings identified by Madison and Kahn over the period up to 1913 do not match Kondratieff's classification indicated in Table 5.1. Both Kahn and Madison classify the period up to 1913 as years of boom, whereas Kondratieff divided the

Table 5.4 *Phases of economic growth in advanced capitalist countries (average output growth p.a. %)*

Phase	Madison (1977)		Kahn (1979)		
I	1870–1913:	2.5	–1885:		'Take-off'
II	1913–1950:	1.9	1886–1913:	3.3	'La belle époque'
III	1950–1970:	4.9	1914–1947:	1.8	'La mauvaise époque'
IV	1970–1976:	3.0	1948–1973:	4.9	'La deuxième, belle époque'
V			1974–2000?	3.5	'L'époque de malaise'

period into sub-periods of slump and boom respectively. However, the main purpose of citing Table 5.4 is that Madison's phases II and III and Kahn's phases III and IV constitute a complete cycle consisting of a protracted slump followed by a protracted boom that has all the appearance of a Kondratieff long wave. Then, right on cue, the postwar boom is followed by what Kahn calls *'l'époque de malaise'*. The timing is uncanny. It has already been argued above that the statistical basis for the Kondratieff analysis is open to question. Indeed, it is ironic that evidence for Kondratieff becomes more telling after 1920, i.e. after the long waves were 'discovered'. A single swallow does not make a summer; nor does a single long wave (1920–70) prove a theory. However, the matter shall not be left there. In the rest of this chapter we will consider critically some of the theoretical arguments that have been proposed for the existence of long waves.

Schumpeter

Schumpeter's original theory of long waves appeared in German in 1911, i.e. before Kondratieff's discovery. The English version of his theory was published in Schumpeter (1934) and this was followed by a massive two-volume empirical analysis of his ideas in Schumpeter (1939). His central theoretical proposition was that economic innovation is essentially discontinuous and that this discontinuity generates fairly long economic cycles. He emphasised the distinction between invention and scientific discovery on the one hand, which concerns the advancement of knowledge, and innovation, on the other hand, which concerns the exploitation of this knowledge for economic gain. Therefore Schumpeter does not propose that there is a cycle to inventiveness. If there is, it is entirely fortuitous and his theory would still apply even if inventions and scientific discovery occurred smoothly over time.

And by innovation he refers to the establishment of 'new combinations'. It is sometimes thought that this in turn refers to the application of new technology such as electrification, computerisation, etc. However, Schumpeter takes a much broader view and 'new combinations' embrace the following:

- new goods or new quality goods
- new methods of production
- new markets
- new supplies of raw material
- new organisation of industry

Therefore, innovation may take place independently of technology and scientific discovery.

Schumpetrian dynamics may be broken down into a number of distinct phases:

(1) Pioneering: individual entrepreneurs, usually relatively few in number launch a new economic activity. Quite often the basic idea has been around for a while but nobody has plucked up the courage to try it out. Quite often these pioneering entrepreneurs fail and are forced into bankruptcy. If, however, they are successful they manage to reap quasi rents since they are first in the field and face either little or no competition.

(2) Swarming: having broken the ice and having demonstrated that the 'new combination' is feasible, the breach that the pioneers have opened is swiftly filled by other entrepreneurs. These entrepreneurs are motivated by the quasi rents that are earned by the pioneers. A central cyclical feature of Schumpeter's theory is that there is a swarming of entrepreneurs during this stage, i.e. they do not gradually invest in the

innovation. Instead the swarming process makes for economic discontinuity and triggers an investment boom during which wages, prices and interest rates tend to rise. The swarming is brought about as each secondary entrepreneur wishes to take advantage of the high quasi rents of the pioneers.

(3) Gestation: while the 'new combinations' are being developed the 'old combinations' continue to survive in the market place. Indeed, for a while old and new products may coexist; valve radios may be sold in the same shops that are selling transistor sets. This coexistence reflects the quasi rents earned by the pioneers who charge the going price for radio sets but whose costs are considerably lower than their counterparts who produce valve sets.

This coexistence comes to an end once the investments of the secondary entrepreneurs have gestated. At this point there is a flood of transistor sets on to the market and the quasi rents are wiped out. At the same time the old combinations fail and are out competed in the market place. As the old combinations fail the boom comes to an end and the economy goes into a slump.

The severity of the slump relative to the boom depends on the intensity of the swarming in Stage 2. The time span of the boom depends on the length of the gestation period. The longer the gestation period, the longer the overall length of the cycle.

(4) Maturity: once the old combinations have been entirely replaced by the innovations a new equilibrium is reached and the slump comes to an end. In this equilibrium living standards are higher as the quasi rents are now consumed by society as a whole. The mature phase is eventually disturbed by yet another generation of pioneers, and so society progresses.

There is nothing in what Schumpeter had to say that would justify the Kondratieff waves, unless empirically it so happened that the gestation period was roughly twenty-five years. This would tend to induce a fifty-year cycle in economic activity. However, gestation periods are unlikely to be so long, and Schumpeter himself seemed to be more concerned with the Juglar (nine-year) cycle that had been previously identified in the nineteenth century.

Unfortunately there has been little study of the innovation process, although Schmookler (1966) provides a thorough study of the relationship between invention and economic growth. He concludes:

> Despite the popularity of the idea that scientific discoveries and major inventions typically provide the stimulus for innovation, the historical record . . . revealed not a single, unambiguous instance in which either discoveries or inventions played the role hypothesized. Instead, in hundreds of cases the stimulus was the recognition of a costly problem to be solved or a potentially profitable opportunity to be seized; in short, a technical problem or opportunity evaluated in economic terms. In a few cases, sheer accident was credited (p. 199).

Of course the basic scientific knowledge must already exist but more often than not the constraint is the market rather than ignorance.

Schmookler's results support Schumpeter on the distinction between invention and innovation, but they shed no light on:

● the swarming hypothesis, and
● the aggregate gestation period.

Table 5.5 records the time distribution of the great innovations of the twentieth century, dated according to their first commercial application or prototype. On the basis of this table the 1930s should have witnessed a Schumpetrian boom and the 1960s should have been recessed for two reasons:

● because of the deceleration in innovation, and
● because the innovations of the previous two decades should have gestated producing a Schumpetrian slump.

This admittedly slender evidence suggests that the Schumpetrian slump in fact came a decade too late, i.e. in the 1970s rather than 1960s. This leads us to conclude that despite its

Table 5.5   *Great innovations 1900–69*

	Number
1900–09	5
1910–19	6
1920–29	5
1930–39	15
1940–49	15
1950–59	10
1960–69	4

Source: Jewkes *et al.* (1969)

intuitive appeal the Schumpetrian analysis is unlikely to provide a theoretical justification for Kondratieff long waves. In
particular, it does not offer any obvious insights into the
causes of the world slump since the late 1960s.

During the 1970s there has been a new generation of
research into the Schumpetrian thesis that has been usefully
reviewed in Freeman (ed) (1981) and which focuses on the
timing and nature of innovations. Using data similar to that
in Table 5.5, Mensch (1979) argues that innovation has
tended to occur during depressions whereas Freeman and
others have cited evidence that innovations are concentrated
during recovery stages. To some extent these disagreements
can be reconciled by drawing the distinction between product (Mensch) and process innovations. The former are concerned with the development of new products whereas the
latter are concerned with the development of new productive processes for existing products. However, it is not made
clear why depressions should trigger product innovations or
why recovery stages should trigger process innovations. In
the latter case it is also necessary to establish why the recovery takes place, since it is this that drives the cycle of innovation. This appears to reverse the Schumpetrian theory,
which argued that the innovation cycle drives the economic
cycle and not the other way about as Schmookler's evidence
suggested.

Apart from the *ad hoc* theorising this new generation of
research has been sterile, because the empirical base has
been too short. For the most part the depression–trigger
thesis is based on the interwar experience and the recov-

ery–trigger thesis is based on the 1950s and 1960s. Such empirical analyses can be no more than anecdotal and cannot provide the basis for a long wave theory. They tell us more about the innovation process than they do about the generation of long waves.

Kuznets

The Kuznets Cycle is based on demography rather than innovation. Kuznets' approach was also much more empirical, his starting point being the discovery of a twenty-year cycle in the US economy. His theory or explanation for these cycles begins with the waves of immigration into the US which, he argues, triggered economic booms. Immigration and associated population growth leads to construction booms as the demand for housing increases. He goes on to identify other leading sectors in the boom and the leading sectors in the slump that emerge once the housing stock has adjusted to its new equilibrium level.

Kuznets did not propose his analysis as a theory giving rise to systematic cycles in countries apart from the US. Nevertheless it is interesting to note, as Table 5.6 shows, that Madison's boom years (summarised in Table 5.4) coincide with periods of rapid population growth, while his slump years coincide with periods of relatively low population growth. Naturally, it is difficult to disentangle cause and effect since economic growth may foster higher birth rates

Table 5.6   *Population and economic growth 1870–1976 (% p.a.)*

	Phase	Output	Population
I:	1870–1913 (Boom)	2.5	1.0
II:	1913–1950 (Slump)	1.9	0.8
III:	1950–1970 (Boom)	4.9	1.1
IV:	1970–1976 (Slump)	3.0	0.6

Source: Madison (1977)

along Malthusian lines. If, instead, it is assumed that population growth is autonomous, it seems reasonable to assume that economic growth will reflect population growth. Therefore part of the downturn in economic growth since the late 1960s most probably reflects demographic factors, while future growth prospects to some extent depend on demographic projections.

Therefore we can accept Kuznets' analysis without agreeing that there are regular long waves in economic life. If, fortuitously, there was a fifty-year cycle (or any other cycle) in population growth there would be a comparable cycle in economic activity.

Rostow

In a series of recent books, Rostow (1978, 1979, 1980) has argued that industrialised countries have indeed been enmeshed in a Kondratieff slump. However, unlike Kondratieff, who was concerned with overall price movements, Rostow has attached importance to relative price movements. His thesis may be summarised as follows:

(1) Shocks to the world economy may come in many forms e.g. demographic, innovations, wars, etc. In this regard his theory is eclectic.

(2) Specific shocks will affect relative prices. Rostow attaches particular significance to relative price movements between manufactures, food and raw materials.

(3) These shocks also affect different sectors of the economy disproportionately, giving rise to a leading sector analysis which echoes his earlier theories about economic growth (Rostow, 1960).

(4) The cause of the economic cycle is relative price of oscillation in the raw materials which in turn reflects perpetual over- and under-shooting of supply and demand in the markets for manufactures, food and raw materials. According to Rostow, boom years are associated with declining relative prices for raw materials since they lower industrial costs, while rising relative raw materials prices affect industrial output adversely, thereby generating slumps.

(5)   Hence producers the world over never manage to co-
      ordinate their investment and production plans.
      Although Rostow does not put it in these terms, there
      is perpetual market failure. The long cycle applies to
      the relative output of manufacturing and basic raw
      materials.

Rostow identifies five trend periods as shown in Table 5.7,
the first two-and-a-half of which roughly match the waves
identified by Kondratieff (Table 5.1), although there are
exceptions. He argues that his theory does not necessarily
suggest regular cycles but a process of oscillatory adjustments to the shocks referred to above. The boom in Phase
IV coincides with a period of declining relative commodity
prices, while the slump of Phase V coincides with rising relative commodity prices. Figure 5.8 shows the relationship
between some of Rostow's trend periods and the relative
price of manufactures, and it is clear that a broad correspondence exists. However, as Spraos (1980) has emphasised, great care must be taken in interpreting such relative
price series. Nevertheless, Spraos' review of the data broadly
supports the picture represented by Figure 5.8.

According to the Transition Theory there is indeed a relationship between economic activity and the relative price of
manufactures. Moreover, the postwar boom and slump
reflect to a large degree the behaviour of these relative price
movements. Where the theory parts company with Rostow
is with his argument that cycles (of even an approximate
nature) will be induced. Why exactly we should all make the
same mistakes over time and refuse to learn is never made
clear by Rostow. He simply takes it for granted that alter-
nate over- and under-shooting in investment and production

Table 5.7   *Rostovian trend periods 1790–1972*

Period	Slump	Boom	Years
I	1790–1815	1815–1848	58
II	1848–1873	1873–1896	48
III	1896–1920	1920–1933	37
IV	1933–1951	1951–1972	39
V	1972–?		

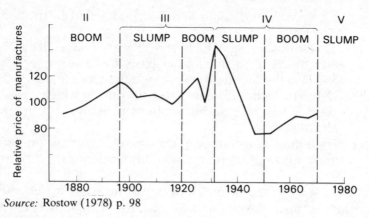

Figure 5.8 *The price of manufactures relative to primary products 1876–1972*

goes on indefinitely. On this basis an energy glut will inevitably emerge following OPEC oil price hikes, the recovery of commodity prices in the 1970s will lead to a glut of raw materials, etc.

This may be so, but it implies market failure of a fundamental kind and implies that markets are always out of equilibrium. To some extent it is a matter of taste whether such assumptions are acceptable. On the other hand, there is a large body of evidence, e.g. Labys and Granger (1970), which strongly suggests that commodity markets are at least weakly efficient and which conflicts with Rostow's perspective. In chapters 2 and 3 relative commodity prices were discussed and their relationship with the level of economic activity within an equilibrium framework. We do not have to resort to the extreme assumptions of Rostow to be able to tell a plausible story. Moreover, these simpler assumptions rule out Rostovian cycles.

Our criticism that Rostovian dynamics do not have strong theoretical underpinnings mirrors the criticism frequently levelled at his 'stages' thesis of economic growth (described in Rostow, 1960). According to this thesis the transition from underdevelopment to development may be broken down into several distinct phases.

(i)   Pre take-off: during which agricultural improvements

take place, and commercial attitudes and institutions develop.

(ii) Take-off: during which the share of investment in GDP rises on a substantial basis for several decades and lays the foundations for modern economic growth.

(iii) Drive to technological maturity: during which investment is less intense but modern technology is gradually absorbed.

(iv) High mass consumption: during which living standard and consumption patterns attain modern proportions.

These stages may or may not be useful ways for characterising *ex post* developments, just as phases of relative prices may or may not be useful in characterising *ex post* economic cycles. The criticism is that there is no aerodynamic theory according to which all economies necessarily pass through these stages. For example why after Stage (ii) will economies remain airborne instead of crashing to the ground? Therefore the 'stages' thesis is no more than an *ex post* system of data classification; it is not an *ex ante* theory of economic growth. The same applies to the Rostovian thesis of long cycles; it is a framework for data classification that may have some appeal to the economic historian but which is of little value to economists attempting to project contemporary economic trends.

The criticism of perpetual over- and under-shooting may be also levelled against the thesis of van Duijn (1977), who has argued that fifty-year cycles may be induced along the following lines:

(1) Major or basic innovations occur in clusters along Schumpetrian lines, giving rise to new industrial sectors.

(2) These sectors raise the demand for infrastructure and capital equipment.

(3) This triggers a multiplier-accelerator process which causes the capital stock to overshoot its steady-state value.

(4) The excess supply of capital is further exacerbated when the demand from the new sectors (now no longer new) levels off.

(5) The excess supply of capital induces an investment-led recession.

(6) Recovery sets in when replacement investment picks up and the multiplier-accelerator starts operating in an upward direction.

(7) As investment recovers the scene is set for a further burst of innovation.

(8) And so the cycle is repeated.

Thus the cycle is essentially an implication of the multiplier-accelerator process and in this sense it is very similar in character to the Rostovian cycle. Of course it would be fortuitous for such a dynamic model to generate a fifty-year cycle and in this sense the long cycle is quite arbitrary. But this is not the central criticism. The central criticism is that the model implies sub-optimal behaviour on the part of consumers and producers who do not exploit the profits that might be earned by smoothing out the cycles. Alternatively, if it is possible to forecast a capital glut rational agents will take evasive action in advance and the price of capital goods will fall in advance and capital supply will fall in anticipation of the glut. Likewise, if a capital shortage is forecast the price of capital goods will rise in advance and capital supply will rise in anticipation of the shortage. The net effect of this anticipatory behaviour is to smooth out the cycle. If gluts and shortages were entirely predictable the smoothing process would be complete.

Thus van Duijn's and Rostow's thesis abstracts from rational economic behaviour and the stabilising influence of market forces under the assumption that expectations are rational. This criticism essentially extends Lucas's (1972) analysis in which rational expectations theory radically transforms conventional business cycle theory. This does not necessarily rule out the possibility of cycles of either short or long duration. Rather, it implies that the long wave analyses discussed in this chapter are incomplete unless, of course, one is prepared to abstract from rational economic behaviour.

The Club of Rome

There have always been fears that the depletion of natural resources is bound to bring modern economic growth to an end. Writing in 1866 the great Victorian economist, William Stanley Jevons, predicted that the industrial revolution in England would be reversed by the end of the century, because coal supplies would be depleted. After the Second World War it was commonly thought that oil reserves would be adequate for no more than twenty-five years and that mass oil production would be no more than a passing phenomenon. Today there are numerous pessimistic forecasts regarding the adequacy of world oil reserves and predictions (e.g. by Eden *et al.*, 1981) of an energy 'crunch' before the century is out, i.e. not unlike Jevons.

This thesis was revived in broader terms by Meadows *et al.* (1972), who concluded that the world is depleting its natural resources and polluting itself to the point where modern economic growth is being threatened. Their work (which was sponsored by the Club of Rome) assumed resources would be consumed at exponential rates over time and since our planet is finite the world must deplete itself into stagnation. Their doomwatch model implied that the 'crunch' would come in the early part of the next century.

This thesis has come in for very widespread criticism, e.g. Cole (1973). The basic point is that the analysis could have been conducted in 1872 with predictions of collapse in the early part of the twentieth century and that, given present knowledge, it will always look as though the world is about to come to an end, just in the same way as the 'flat earthers' thought travel was dangerous. But knowledge is not a constant and never has been. Nor is it likely to be in the future. It would, of course, be a contradiction in terms to predict how future knowledge will develop, but this does not justify zero knowledge growth as a neutral assumption. In any case, even if resources are finite, market forces will provide plenty of advance warning since the prices of these resources will rise gradually over time (according to the rate of discount), e.g. Heal and Dasgupta (1979), so that economic change will take place in advance of the crisis. The thesis that society will be taken by surprise ignores the existence of markets.

The reason for mentioning the Club of Rome thesis largely reflects the coincidence of its publication date with the onset of the present recession. Even though the 'crisis' was supposed to be fifty years away it was argued in many quarters that the crisis had already started. However, our argument has been that this was indeed no more than a coincidence and that it has no substantiative significance. Had the publication date been 1932 or 1886 we would have not bothered to mention it. Commentators in the next century will most probably refer to Meadows *et al.* (1972) as contemporary commentators refer to Jevons (1866).

Summary

We reject the Club of Rome thesis as an explanation of the recession and we reject Rostow's thesis that the recession is an inevitable consequence of Kondratieff forces. More fundamentally, we question the statistical as well as the theoretical bases for Kondratieff waves. The recession which began in the late 1960s may have been inevitable for other reasons but there are no historicist forces which dictate that economic history must repeat itself even in the broadest of terms.

6

Transition in the Nineteenth Century: The British Climacteric 1860–1900

Introduction

An important thesis was proposed in Chapters 3 and 4, namely that the world economy is in a state of transition and that industrialisation in developing countries has been causing relative prices to shift, which has brought about economic restructuring in the industrialised countries. The central argument in this chapter is that this process has happened before. During the second half of the nineteenth century the economic rise of the US, Germany, Russia and France posed the same kind of threat for Britain that developing countries are posing a century later for the OECD bloc. Naturally, the precise details are not the same but the parallel is striking.

As the first country to industrialise, Britain was the most important economic power in the world by the mid-nineteenth century. She accounted for about 30 per cent of world industrial production (using the figures in Rostow, 1978, p. 52), 25 per cent of world trade (Rostow, 1978, p. 70), and only 1.7 per cent of world population. By 1900, the former proportions had fallen to 15 per cent and 16 per cent respectively. The juxtaposition of the British economy and the rest of the world in 1850 is strikingly similar to the relationship between the industrialised countries and the developing countries just over a hundred years later. Apart from its economic dominance, Britain largely imported raw materials and exported manufactures, just as the industrial-

Table 6.1 *Share of manufactures in trade in Britain and industrialised countries (%)*

	Britain 1850[a]	Industrialised countries 1970[b]
Exports	80	78
Imports	5.5 (1860)	26
		14 (1959)

Sources: a. Deane and Cole (1962) Tables 9 and 10
        b. Batchelor *et al.* (1980) Table 2.3

ised countries did a century or so later as shown in Table 6.1.

Economic historians generally recognise that during the second half of the nineteenth century the British economy underwent a climacteric from which it has never recovered, even today. The period 1873–95 was considered to be the original Great Depression, reflecting the more or less persistent price deflation over this period. There has been much argument over the timing of this climacteric. Phelps Brown and Handfield-Jones (1952) maintain that it was not until the 1890s that the adverse economic change took place. At the other extreme, Coppock (1956) dates it from the 1870s and argues that even in the 1860s there were signs of economic transition. This debate has been reviewed by Saul (1969), who concludes that while transition did indeed take place, sooner rather than later, the Great Depression as such never existed.

I shall lean towards Coppock's position and attempt to explain the climacteric in terms of economic adjustments that were forced on Britain by the rise of industrial competitors. As we shall see, this story is remarkably similar to that which has been unfolding over the last fifteen years or so of the emergence of the developing countries and their relationship with the industrialised countries.

The Climacteric

Table 6.2 provides some key indicators of the level of economic activity during the second half of the nineteenth century. It shows that unemployment was some two points higher over the period 1875–95. In 1879 unemployment

Table 6.2   *Economic growth in Britain 1830–1913 (% per decade)*

	GDP	Industrial production	Unemployment
1830–1860	22.0[a]	51.3[b]	na
1855–1865	28.7	49.6	3.7
1865–1875	24.6	27.3	3.3
1875–1885	14.7	11.5	5.6
1885–1895	23.7	13.8	5.7
1895–1905	23.9	30.8	3.7
1905–1913	22.7	22.1	4.5

Sources: Feinstein (1972) Tables 54 and 57
a. Deane and Cole (1969) Table 72
b. Rostow (1978) Appendix A

rose to 10.7 per cent and in 1886 it reached 10.2 per cent. Although there was a high degree of variability in the data and although the data are subject to error, it would seem that the labour market was generally depressed during 1875–95.

The data for the rate of growth of industrial production suggest a similar picture. During this period industrial production grew by less than half the average for the century as a whole. This depression is also reflected, but to a smaller degree, in the rate of growth of GDP, which decelerated sharply over the period 1875–85 before recovering to its erstwhile levels.

Note that this identification of recession is based on real indicators of economic activity. This is in sharp contrast to Kondratieff who, as noted in Chapter 5, based his analysis on price rather than quantity indicators. These indicators seem to support Coppock's view that the climacteric occurred around 1870 rather than around 1890, as Phelps Brown and Handfield-Jones have argued.

Transition Theory

The Transition Theory described in Chapter 3 had the following essential elements:

(1)   Industrial growth takes place in the periphery. In the present context the periphery consists of the US, Germany, France and Russia.

(2)   This growth adversely affects the relative price of manufactures and/or threatens the trading power of the core. In the present context the core consists of Britain.

(3)   The new set of relative prices and/or the trade threat to the core on the part of the periphery causes de-industrialisation in the core as the share of industrial production in GDP declines from what it otherwise would have been.

(4)   This in turn raises the wage share, reduces the profit share and adversely affects the return on capital in the core.

(5)   The lower returns to capital cause a reduction of investment in the core and increased foreign investment by the core in the periphery.

(6)   While de-industrialisation takes place there is a temporary if protracted period of mismatch unemployment and slower economic growth in the core.

The thesis of this chapter is that the climacteric can largely be understood in terms of the Transition Theory. In this sense, the climacteric was a preview of the transition that is presently (since about 1970) taking place, where the core consists of the OECD bloc and the periphery consists of the LDCs. However, as we shall see, the theory is not a perfect fit and there are a number of loose ends. Nevertheless in most respects the Transition Theory fits the facts closely and the evidence as a whole is supportive of the basic thesis.

The role of foreign competition in the climacteric has been noted by Coppock (1956) and has been closely studied by Aldcroft (1968). Attention to this phenomenon was first drawn by Lewis (1949). Subsequently Lewis (1978b) has argued that while the climacteric was induced by foreign competition it was only a necessary and not a sufficient condition for decline, since Britain could have moved up market by taking advantage of the new science-based industries that emerged during the second industrial revolution of the latter part of the nineteenth century. Britain's failure to adapt reflected the rigidities imposed on the labour market by growing trade unionisation and the snobbery on the part of the upper classes, who did not understand the need for technological and vocational education upon which the new industries would be based. Lewis (1978b, p. 133) sums up the situation as follows:

> Thus Britain was caught in a set of ideological traps. All the strategies available to her were blocked off in one way or another. She could not lower costs by cutting wages because of the unions, or switch to American-type technology because of the slow pace of British workers. She could not reduce her propensity to import by imposing a tariff or by devaluing her currency, or increase her propensity to export by devaluing or by paying export subsidies. She could not pioneer in developing new commodities because this now required a scientific base which did not accord with her humanistic snobbery.
>
> So instead she invested her savings abroad; the economy decelerated, the average level of unemployment increased and her young people emigrated.

The Transition Theory is, in many respects, an elaboration and extension of Lewis's and Coppock's analysis. Certainly it, too, takes as its starting point industrialisation in the periphery. Thereafter, however, there are some important differences.

The Evidence

(1)   The Periphery

During the first half of the nineteenth century industrial production in the periphery (represented by the US, France and Germany) grew at an average annual rate of approximately 2.9 per cent. During the second half of the century this rate of growth increased to 4.25 per cent. Figure 6.1 provides a more graphic impression of the acceleration of industrial production during the latter decades of the century. It should be recalled that these data exclude Russia and other peripheral countries where industrialisation took place at this time, although perhaps to a less marked degree. Indeed, just as today the periphery of developing countries has perhaps a first, a second and even a third division,

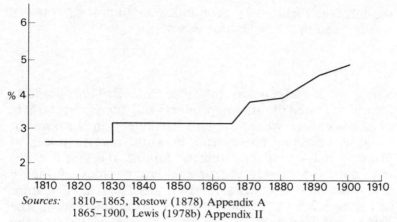

Sources: 1810–1865, Rostow (1878) Appendix A
           1865–1900, Lewis (1978b) Appendix II

Figure 6.1   *Growth of industrial production in the USA, France and Germany 1810–1910 (% p.a., annual averages)*

reflecting individual countries' state of development, so the periphery in the last century was heterogeneous too.

Unfortunately, aggregate data are not readily available on the distribution of economic growth in the periphery. For example, we cannot readily compare the growth of industrial production with the growth of output as a whole. Therefore we cannot infer whether industrialisation in the periphery was concentrated in the manufacturing sector. Nevertheless Table 6.3 provides some rough indication of the relative performance of the industrial sector in the periphery. During the second half of the nineteenth century it would appear that the share of industrial production in GDP rose quite sharply, especially in Germany and the US. Therefore at a time when the share of industrial production decelerated in

Table 6.3   *The share of industry in GDP in the periphery 1789–1920*

France		Germany		Canada		USA		Sweden	
1789–1815	20								
1825–1835	25					1839	28		
1872–1882	30	1860–1869	24	1870	26	1879	51	1861–1865	17
1908–1910	37	1905–1914	39	1920	35			1901–1905	38

Source: Kuznets (1960) Table 3.1

the UK (see Figure 6.4), economic growth in the periphery was focused in the industrial sector.

(2)   Relative Prices

Since, as already noted in Table 6.1, Britain's imports largely consisted of primary products and her exports largely of manufactures, we may regard movements in her terms of trade as reflecting movements in world relative prices of primary and secondary products. Indeed, the first decades of Figure 6.5 closely mirror the last decades of Figure 6.2, which plots Britain's terms of trade. The striking feature of Figure 6.2 is the halving of the terms of trade during the first half of the nineteenth century. This implies that over the period the relative price of primary products to secondary products more or less doubled. This largely reflected falling prices of British cotton exports, which in turn reflected technological innovation.

During the second half of the century the terms of trade improved, which implies that the British climacteric took place against a background of falling rather than rising relative primary product prices. This aspect of the data contradicts Stage 2 of the Transition Theory, although, as noted above, we do not know whether the economic expansion in the periphery increased the net excess supply of manufac-

Source: Imlah (1958)

Figure 6.2   *British terms of trade 1796–1913 (1913 = 100)*

tures. The other interpretation of Stage 2 is that, even in the absence of relative price shifts, the core may face direct competition in international trade by the periphery. This is clearly indicated by Figure 6.3. During the last decades of the eighteenth century there was a very marked expansion in the British trade share. In view of data inadequacies the peak on Figure 6.3 should be regarded as no more than a qualitative impression of this transformation. After some decline in the early part of the nineteenth century, the trade share remained relatively steady between 1830 and 1870. Thereafter the trade share declined steadily, although the break in the series most probably overstates the loss of trade share. Note that this decline coincides with the acceleration of industrial growth in the periphery that was identified under Stage 1.

There is, of course, no reason why the trade share should remain constant. If the British economy becomes smaller relative to the world economy, it is only natural that the trade share should decline. Figure 6.3 shows that this is what happened. The British share of 'world' industrial production, which had been relatively steady, for about a century declined sharply after 1870. Nevertheless Table 6.4 strongly suggests that increased industrial competitiveness in the

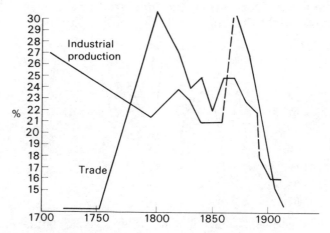

Source: Rostow (1978) Tables II-2, II-8 and Appendix A

Figure 6.3 *British share of world trade and industrial production 1700–1913 (%)*

Table 6.4   *Growth of export volumes in Britain 1841–1910 (% p.a.)*

1841–1870	4.9
1870–1880	3.4
1880–1890	2.6
1890–1900	0.5
1900–1910	3.9

Sources: Feinstein (1982) Table 7; Deane and Cole (1969) Table 83

periphery sharply reduced the rate of growth of UK exports. Certainly, British exports suffered over the period that the peripheral growth accelerated. This evidence therefore tends to confirm Stage 2 of the Transition Theory.

(3)   De-industrialisation

In this stage, competition from abroad which has adversely affected exports causes the share of industrial production in GDP to decline. This phenomenon is shown in Figure 6.4 and the timing is right on cue. Between approximately 1830 and 1855, the share of industrial production in GDP had been rising sharply. Figure 6.4 indicates an abrupt break in this trend after 1870 so that in the early 1890s, i.e. at the end of the Great Depression, the industrial production share is approximately the same as it was thirty years before.

Source: Feinstein (1972) Table 54

Figure 6.4   *The ratio of industrial production to GDP in Britain 1700–1913 (1913 = 100)*

Figure 6.5 reminds us that such bouts of stagnation in the industrial production share had happened before. Between 1831 and 1851 the rate was more or less zero after having grown dramatically over the previous two decades. Since the data in Figure 6.5 are calculated at current prices the share will reflect relative price movements between manufactures and goods in general. In this context we already know from Figure 6.2 that during the first half of the century there were substantial falls in relative prices, especially after 1820. Therefore the chart may not necessarily reflect relative resource shifts into and out of the industrial sector. Nevertheless, where Figures 6.4 and 6.5 overlap in time there is a rough correspondence between the data, with the 1850s and the 1860s being decades of rapid relative industrialisation followed by a decline in the 1870s and 1880s.

Further evidence for de-industrialisation is shown in Figure 6.6 which plots the industrial allocation of employment. During the 1840s and 1850s the allocation of employment to the industrial sector had been growing. After 1861 this ratio ceased to grow for three decades, so that the allocation in 1891 was about the same as in 1861. Like Figure 6.4, Figure 6.6 suggests that the seeds of the climacteric were laid in the 1860s, thus supporting Coppock's thesis.

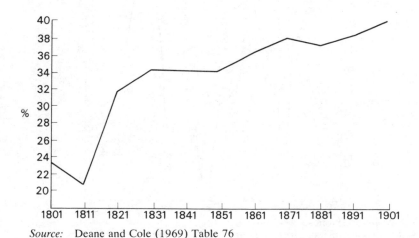

Source: Deane and Cole (1969) Table 76

Figure 6.5 *Manufactures, mining and building as a percentage of national income in Britain 1801–1901*

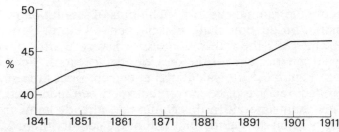

Source: Deane and Cole (1969) Table 30

Figure 6.6   *The share of industrial employment in Britain 1841–1911 (%)*

(4)   Income Distribution

According to the Transition Theory the de-industrialisation in Stage 3 should be accompanied by a decline in the profit share in Stage 4. Figure 6.7 bears this out. The profit share (including income from self-employment) peaked in 1871, after which it went into a protracted decline which did not come to an end until the end of the 1890s. In other words, the decline in the profit share coincides more or less exactly

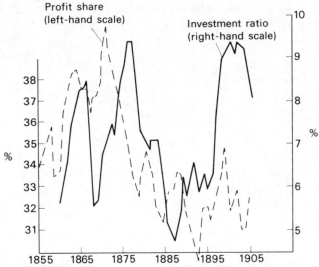

Sources: Profit share: Feinstein (1972) Table 18
Investment ratio: Deane and Cole (1969) Table 91

Figure 6.7   *Investment and profit shares in Britain 1855–1905 (% of GDP)*

with the Great Depression and the onset of the climacteric. Its timing is also right on cue as far as the Transition Theory is concerned.

(5) Investment

Unfortunately, data on the rate of return to capital are not readily available, although it seems probable that Figure 6.7 is consistent with a fall in the rate of return to capital in the core during the 1870s and 1880s. In addition, it is probable that the industrialisation in the periphery had the effect of raising the rate of return on capital in these countries, although here too it is difficult to forward the necessary evidence.

A lower rate of return on capital in the core would tend to reduce proportionate investment and savings. However, if this is accompanied by a rise in the return on capital in the periphery, the savings ratio need not fall as investors in the core channel their investment from the core to the periphery. Figure 6.8 shows that the savings ratio tended to rise, even during the 1880s; there is no indication that the declining profit share adversely affected the propensity to save. In contrast, Figure 6.7 indicates that domestic capital

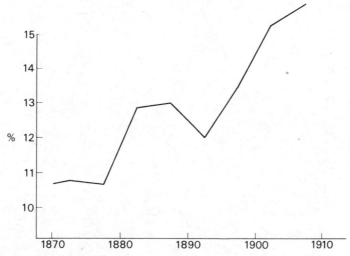

Source: Feinstein (1972) Table 19

Figure 6.8 *The savings ratio in Britain 1870–1910*

formation, which had been on an upward trend up to the mid-1870s, declined markedly over the period 1877–1898. Indeed the chart suggests that there is lagged positive relationship between the investment ratio and the profit share. This could reflect the Kaldorian 'Widow's Cruise' thesis that an increase in the investment ratio raises the profit share. However, the lag in the data suggests that the causal flow goes from the profit share to investment rather than the other way round, i.e. along neoclassical rather than neo-Keynesian lines.

Figure 6.9 shows that apart from 1876–80 net capital outflows on the British balance of payments were unusually high, averaging at times 7 per cent of GDP. In contrast, during the first half of the century this ratio was typically zero. Therefore during the second half of the century and especially after 1865, Britain became a very large capital exporter. Thus it seems that, while the domestic investment ratio declined, the net outward foreign investment ratio rose to such a degree that the savings ratio increased instead of declining.

Figure 6.10 illustrates the nature of British capital exports between 1865 and 1913. The investment was largely concentrated on the development of social overhead capital in

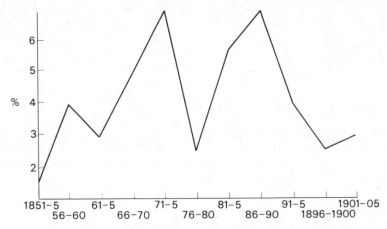

Source: Net capital balance, Deane and Cole (1969) Table 11
               GDP Feinstein (1972) Table 1

Figure 6.9   *Net capital outflow as a percentage of GDP in Britain 1851–1905*

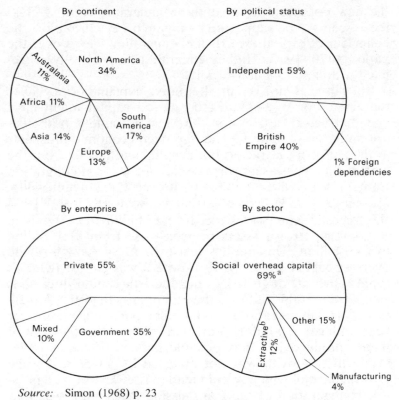

Source: Simon (1968) p. 23
Note: a. includes transportation, public utilities and public works
      b. includes agriculture and mining

Figure 6.10 *The distribution of British portfolio investment abroad 1865–1914*

the North American private sector. The manufacturing sector took only 4 per cent of the outward investment. From this point of view it would seem that there is a significant difference in the composition of capital exports between the core in the nineteenth century and the core in the twentieth century. In the latter case private capital exports have been predominantly targeted on the manufacturing sector. An alternative explanation for capital exports from Britain is that emigration from Britain to the US generated complementary exports of capital. Thus, when emigration increased, the emigrants either took their capital with them or British capital followed in their wake to take advantage of the new opportunities that these emigrants created. This thesis seems to be supported by Figure 6.11, which plots the behaviour of capital exports and emigration waves over the period 1870–1913. Higher emigration is positively correlated with larger capital exports.

But this may not be an alternative explanation, because the emigration of human and physical capital might have been induced by a common third factor, namely industrialisation in the periphery. The improved economic prospects in the periphery attracted both capital and labour from the core and it comes as no surprise that the wave of emigration from 1875 to 1895 coincided with the Great Depression. Cairncross (1953) estimates that between 1875 and 1914 the domestic capital stock rose from £5 billion to £9.2 billion. In contrast, British assets overseas rose from £1.1 billion to £4.0 billion. This implies that the rate of growth of the overseas capital stock (British owned) was almost twice as rapid as the rate of growth of the domestic capital stock. It is estimated that this reduced the rate of growth of the domestic capital–labour ratio by about half a percentage point per year, with corresponding reductions in the rate of growth of labour productivity. It is possible that, in so far as lower productivity growth was not matched by lower real wage growth, unemployment would tend to rise. Therefore a possible configuration of the transmission mechanism was that capital exports reduced real wage growth and/or increased

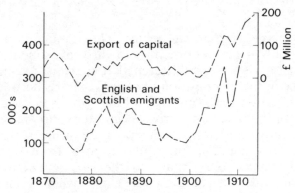

Source: Cairncross (1953) p. 212

Figure 6.11   *Emigration and capital exports from Britain 1870–1913*

unemployment, which in turn generated the wave of emigration after 1875.

(6) Recession

This completes the circle of the Transition Thesis and brings us back to Table 6.2, where data covering the Great Depression and the associated climacteric were presented. The main inference is that these phenomena were brought about by economic growth in the periphery in accordance with the Transition Theory. The deceleration of industrialisation that was brought about by foreign competition had the effect of generating mismatch unemployment and recession in the core. Table 6.2 testifies to the higher unemployment and the recession but lack of data prevents us from determining where the recession was most pronounced. According to the Transition Theory it should be in the manufacturing and traded goods sectors that the recession had its greatest effect.

Summary

The British economic climacteric that occurred during the second half (and especially the last three decades) of the nineteenth century may be understood in terms of the Transition Theory. The chronology of events broadly matches the stages of this theory as shown on Figure 6.12 where the principal causal relationships are indicated. Note that Figure 6.12 implies that the circular flow is complete, since foreign investment by the core accelerates growth in the periphery, although it is likely to have a stabilising effect on the differential rate of return on capital between the periphery and the core.

The Great Depression lasted about twenty years. Unemployment eventually came down, as Table 6.2 indicates, suggesting that the period of transition was roughly two decades. There is of course no basis to infer from this that transitions necessarily last two decades; it all depends on the scale, duration and composition of the shock waves that emanate from the periphery as well as the economic linkages

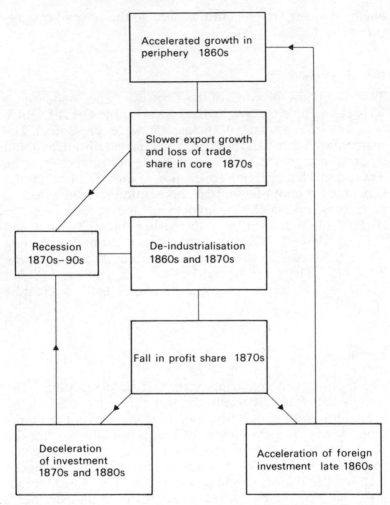

Figure 6.12 *Stages of transition in Britain in the late nineteenth century*

between periphery and core. Instead, the main inference is that the transition that began in the late 1960s has an important antecedent, namely the transition in the late 1860s which had a major bearing on the Great Depression and the economic climacteric in Britain.

7

A Re-run of the 1970s[*]

Three Basic Questions

In this chapter we ask the following questions:

- What would have happened to the industrialised economies in the 1970s had commodity prices not risen as sharply as they did in the early 1970s?
- What would have happened had OPEC not raised oil prices in 1973–4 and then again in 1978–9?
- What would have happened to the industrialised economies had monetary policy behaved in the 1970s as it did in the 1960s when money supply grew at a slower average rate?

The purpose of these questions is to determine how far shocks to commodity prices, oil prices and monetary policy were responsible for the slower growth and higher inflation that OECD countries, taken as a group, experienced in the 1970s relative to the 1960s. Is it the case, for example, that the commodity price explosion that took place during the early 1970s was stagflationary and if so, to what degree? Similarly, what were the effects of the OPEC price hikes upon OECD output and inflation? It would be wrong to suggest that these shocks were independent. However, it is arguable that, even if commodity prices had not taken off during 1972–3, OPEC would in any case have quadrupled oil prices in 1974. On the other hand, it may be argued that the commodity price boom set the scene for the oil price boom

---

[*] This chapter has been jointly written with Geoffrey Dicks.

that followed in its wake, and that but for the commodity price boom the oil price hikes would have been less spectacular than they were. We can say perhaps more definitely that the shocks to monetary policy were not independent, since part of the expansion in monetary growth during the 1970s was a result of policies that accommodated cost-push inflation induced by higher oil and commodity prices. Nevertheless, there are signs that, even before these price shocks (in 1971–2) monetary policy was expansionary.

The Model

To answer these questions we deploy the econometric model of the world economy described by Beenstock and Dicks (1981). This model aggregates the OECD countries; a more technical summary is provided in an appendix to this chapter. The model was estimated from quarterly data over the period 1963Q1 to 1979Q4 and contains the variables listed in Table 7.1. Thus the model is small and highly aggregated, although its tracking performance is impressive. The model abstracts from movements in non-industrial output and the prices of non-manufactures. Therefore it cannot explain the phenomena considered in Chapter 4 which were concerned with relative price and output movements. Nor does it purport to deal with the Transition Theory. Instead, industrial production represents the level of economic activity and wholesale prices are intended to represent the general price level, although we know from Chapter 4 that this is no more than a broad approximation. The present exercise is therefore complementary to the exercise carried out at the end of Chapter 4.

Table 7.1   *Variables in the 'world model'*

Endogenous variables	Exogenous variables
Industrial production	Oil price index
Wholesale prices (manufactures)	
Money supply (broad definition)	
Commodity price index	

The model determines the evolution of the endogenous variables over time for given assumptions about the price of oil, which is assumed to be set by OPEC. The model is dynamic in the sense that shocks take time to die away, so that disturbances reverberate for as long as between three and five years after their initial occurrence. This will become clearer as we illustrate the behaviour of the model below.

In the long run, the level of output is assumed to grow at a constant rate of 4.2 per cent per year. However, higher real oil prices reduce the demand for energy, which in turn depress aggregate supply for reasons described at length in Chapter 2. The model suggests that the long run elasticity of output with respect to real oil prices is -0.088, which implies that the quadrupling of real oil prices permanently lowers the level of industrial production by nearly 12 per cent. This may be compared with the calculations in Chapter 4, which suggested that in the case of output as a whole in the developed countries the quadrupling of oil prices had the estimated effect of reducing output by about 2 per cent. This suggests that the industrial sector is more energy intensive than output as a whole. However, the model failed to identify any adverse supply-side effects of real raw materials prices.

In the long run the demand for money is assumed to vary directly with the level of economic activity and to be proportionate to the price level, i.e. a Quantity Theory framework is postulated, in which the income elasticity of the demand for money is estimated at 1.25. If, in the short run, the demand for money is less than the supply of money, real balance effects are positive and the economy goes into a boom. Conversely, when there is an excess demand for money it goes into a slump as agents save to restore their real balance positions. During booms there is demand-pull inflation, but commodity and oil price movements generate cost-push inflation. But the Quantity Theory framework implies that, once output is at its long run or 'natural' level, the price level is proportionate to the money stock and costs can only exert a temporary influence on the price level. In this respect the model is 'monetarist', although it is clear that supply shocks may affect prices in the short and longer runs.

The supply of money is endogenous and is explained in

terms of a government reaction function. The authorities are assumed to raise monetary growth when output is below its natural level and to reduce it during boom periods. In addition they lower monetary growth as inflation accelerates. Thus the reaction function implies that the authorities regard inflation and slump as undesirables. Finally, commodity prices rise with the price level and the cost of oil since energy is an input into the production of commodities. They also rise when the level of commodity demand is raised by an increase in the level of economic activity in the OECD bloc. The oil price elasticity is 0.39, and the income elasticity is 3.13 in the long run. The model also assumes that the demand for commodities varies directly with expected inflation since they serve as a hedge against inflation.

Simulative Properties of the Model

Although the money supply is endogenous in the model, Figures 7.1 and 7.2 illustrate the consequences of autonomous changes in the supply of money across OECD countries as a whole. In the initial period the money supply is raised permanently by 10 per cent and the simulation is carried out over a ten year period. Figure 7.1 indicates that after about four or five years the OECD price level rises in line with the money supply, although most of the build-up occurs during

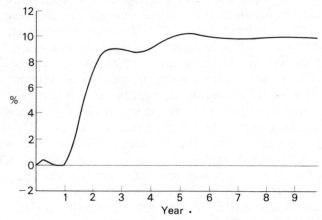

Figure 7.1   *The effect of a 10 per cent increase in the money supply on the price level*

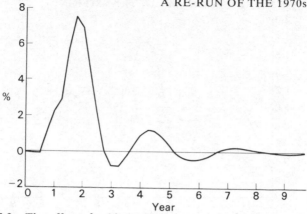

Figure 7.2 *The effect of a 10 per cent increase in the money supply on output*

the second and third years. Notice that during the first year there is almost no price response at all. This supports the view that it takes about eighteen months before monetary policy begins to affect prices.

Figure 7.2 indicates that in the short run the expansion of the money supply expands the level of economic activity, especially during the second year. Towards the end of the second year real income has expanded by almost 8 per cent and the price level by about 6 per cent, so that nominal income has grown by about 14 per cent. This implies that nominal income overshoots its long run equilibrium by a substantial margin but is quickly corrected. The boom is short-lived, so that by the end of the third year output is more or less back to its initial equilibrium. These charts together suggest that the period of adjustment to monetary disturbances in the OECD bloc is approximately four years.

Figures 7.3 and 7.4 illustrate simulations when OPEC is assumed to raise real oil prices by 10 per cent on a permanent basis in the initial period. These simulations assume that the money supply is fixed. The charts indicate that both output and prices are permanently affected. The price level rises by about 1 per cent and output falls by about 0.8 per cent, although it appears that the model has oscillatory properties with a phase of five years. The short-run stagflationary effects of high oil prices build up quite rapidly so that by the end of the first year the full long-term effects are achieved.

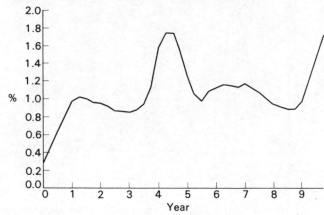

Figure 7.3   *The effect of a 10 per cent increase in the real oil price on the price level*

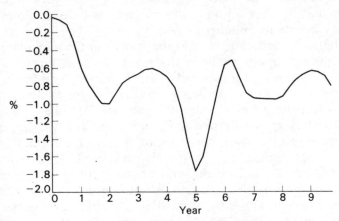

Figure 7.4   *The effect of a 10 per cent increase in the real oil price on output*

Setting-up the Simulations

In considering the effects of the shocks listed at the beginning of this chapter we proceed in the following way. First we set up a base run for the 1970s using actual oil prices and leaving the model to solve for all the endogenous variables in the model including commodity prices, output, money supply and the price level. Figures 7.5 and 7.6 indicate that

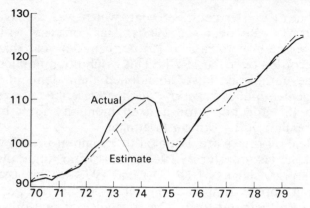

Figure 7.5 *Tracking the level of output 1970–9 (1975 = 100)*

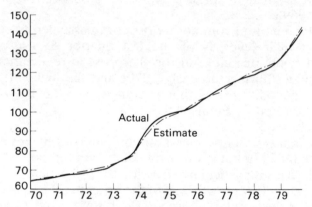

Figure 7.6 *Tracking the price level 1970–9 (1975 = 100)*

for prices and output the base run tracks very well, although
the model underpredicted the level of output over the period
1972–4.

All the simulations that we report below are expressed in
terms of deviations from the base run rather than deviations
from the actual history of the 1970s. But since the base run
is a fairly accurate representation of history this hardly matters. The next step is to construct a 're-run' of the 1970s by
making the following assumptions.

(1) During the 1970s the money supply grows at a constant

rate of $9\frac{1}{2}$ per cent per year, which was the average growth rate over the 1960s. This contrasts with the average growth rate of $13\frac{1}{2}$ per cent per year that was recorded over the 1970s. This assumption implies that the authorities have abandoned their demand management policy-reaction function, described above and in the appendix, for a fixed monetary growth rule popularised by Milton Friedman.

(2) Real oil prices are assumed to remain at their level as of the last quarter of 1969. Apart from ruling out the oil price shocks of 1973–4 and 1978–9, this assumption implies that in 1971 oil prices are 20 per cent below their out-turn. The constancy of real oil prices might prejudice the results because, as Figure 2.7 reveals, real oil prices fell steadily between 1950 and 1969.

(3) Real non-oil commodity prices are assumed to remain at their level as of the last quarter of 1969. This assumption rules out the sharp rise in real commodity prices during the early 1970s and the higher level of commodity prices that prevailed over the 1970s as is indicated by Figure 4.3.

The monetary growth assumption implies a higher rate of growth for 1970 but a lower rate of growth for the rest of the decade. This is particularly true for 1971–3, when the actual rate of monetary growth was of the order of 50 per cent. The results of the simulation are shown in rows 3 and 8 of Table 7.2 and in Figure 7.7. The initial boost to the money supply pushes the price level above the base in 1970, but thereafter prices are lower throughout the period. Figure 7.7 measures the percentage deviations from the base run for the price level and the level of output.

Inflation is reduced, particularly in 1974 and 1979. For the decade as a whole inflation averages 4 per cent, which compares with an out-turn of $8\frac{1}{2}$ per cent and a 1960s average of 2 per cent. By the end of the period, therefore, the price level is some thirty per cent lower than actually recorded. A similar story is revealed for output. Compared with the base run, output is initially higher – because of faster monetary growth and lower oil prices – lower in

Table 7.2 Output and prices 1960–9 and 1970–9 (changes % p.a.)

	1960–9	1970–9	1970	1971	1972	1973	1974	1975	1976	1977	1978	1979	1979 (1975 = 100)	Row number
Output														
History	6.1	3.5	3.2	2.1	6.6	8.9	0.0	–8.0	8.5	4.0	3.9	5.1	123	1
Model tracking		3.5	4.0	1.6	4.9	7.0	3.0	–6.9	6.0	4.9	4.4	5.7	124	2
1960s re-run		4.3	4.0	1.9	5.6	4.4	4.1	4.3	4.2	4.2	4.2	4.2	133	3
Constant real commodity prices		3.5	4.0	1.5	4.7	7.5	3.3	–7.2	5.3	5.0	5.1	5.7	124	4
Constant monetary growth		3.1	4.0	2.1	4.4	3.8	1.7	–6.6	7.6	3.1	4.0	6.7	119	5
Inflation														
History	1.9	8.4	4.4	3.5	3.3	8.5	21.5	8.9	7.4	7.3	5.4	10.5	134	6
Model tracking		8.4	5.2	3.6	4.0	6.7	19.8	10.5	7.7	7.3	6.3	10.0	135	7
1960s re-run		3.9	5.3	3.2	3.3	3.9	4.0	4.0	4.0	4.0	4.0	4.0	92	8
Constant real commodity prices		8.4	5.2	3.8	3.8	6.4	19.9	11.0	7.7	6.9	6.2	10.5	135	9
Constant monetary growth		6.0	5.1	3.8	4.4	4.5	15.2	6.2	5.3	4.6	2.2	7.7	110	10

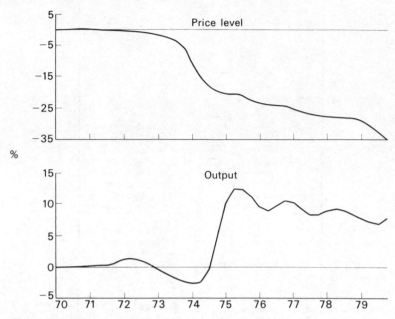

Figure 7.7 *'Re-run' of the 1970s: price level and output*

1973–4 – as the monetary explosion is damped down – and higher from 1975 onwards, as the oil shock is suppressed. For the 1970s as a whole the no-shock scenario would have permitted $4\frac{1}{4}$ per cent per annum growth of output in comparison with $3\frac{1}{2}$ per cent actual growth and 6 per cent in the 1960s. (It is a property of the model that the growth of output slowed in the 1970s for reasons over and above the shocks considered here. For any given rate of growth of the money supply, therefore, the underlying rate of inflation is correspondingly higher.) By the end of the decade the level of output is approximately 10 per cent higher because, as Figure 7.4 revealed, higher oil prices adversely affect the natural level of output. The lower price level reflects both the lower money stock and the higher level of output that is generated by the lower level of real oil prices.

The Effect of Commodity Prices

Given that a no-shock scenario produces for the 1970s a decade similar to the 1960s, it is now possible to assess the

relative contribution to the 1970s' poorer performance of
the three shocks. First we consider what our model tells us
about economic performance in the 1970s in the absence of
a cycle in non-oil commodity prices. (Monetary growth
remains as given by the model and oil prices take their actual
values; the reader should note our earlier remarks on the
interdependence of the three shocks).

In this simulation, real non-oil commodity prices are
unchanged throughout the decade, i.e. commodity prices
grow at exactly the same rate as the price of manufactures.
The results are shown in Table 7.2, rows 4 and 9, and in
Figure 7.8. According to the model, the behaviour of commodity prices has no long run (permanent) effect on the
general price level or even on output. That is, commodity
prices have only a transitory effect, although in the short
term they may be important. Thus if commodity prices had
grown in line with the price of manufactures in 1971 (instead
of falling 2 per cent), inflation would have been slightly
higher and output lower. By the end of 1972, however,
commodity prices were accelerating, and in the course of
1973 they rose by nearly 50 per cent. Again, if this had not
happened, the overall price level would have been lower and
output higher. A similar story persists throughout the
decade, although by 1979 there is no overall effect on either
prices or output.

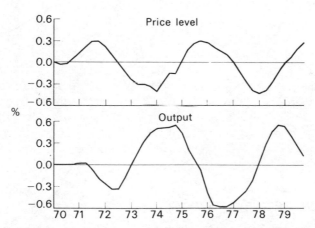

Figure 7.8   *The effect of higher commodity prices on the price level and
output in the 1970s*

The Effect of Oil Prices

If, in terms of our model, commodity prices do not explain the weaker economic performance of the 1970s, we need to consider the contribution of oil prices. This we do in rows 5 and 10 of Table 7.2 and Figure 7.9. In this simulation the money supply grows by $9\frac{1}{2}$ per cent per annum, commodity prices are determined by the model and the oil price takes its actual values. Here the message of the model is quite unambiguous: by the end of the decade the money supply would have been nearly 25 per cent lower as a result of which prices would have been nearly 20 per cent lower and output nearly 5 per cent lower. Most of the effect of a tight monetary policy would have been felt, therefore, on prices, although output would have been permanently lower from 1972 onwards. Once, therefore, the oil shock had taken place, a partly-accommodating monetary policy was able to sustain output at least to some degree.

In terms of our model, therefore – and separating the

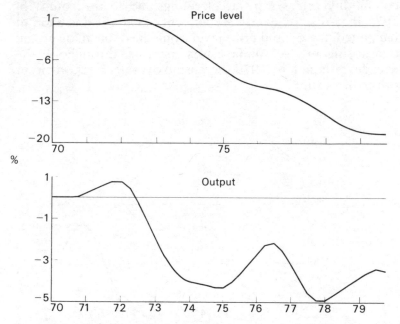

Figure 7.9   *The effect of higher oil prices on the price level and output in the 1970s*

three shocks – we can say that:

- the major upwards influence on prices/downwards influence on output was the 1973–4 quadrupling of oil prices
- non-oil commodity prices, though of importance on a year-by-year basis, had no permanent effect
- monetary policy, by partly accommodating inflation after the oil price shock, also supported output
- in the absence of any shocks, output growth and inflation could have averaged 4 per cent per annum.

Thus, apart from the anti-social pricing policies discussed in Chapter 2, OPEC has been responsible to a large degree for the spiral of worldwide inflation and recession since 1973.

Appendix: The World Model

The Quantity Theory

We postulate a world demand for money function of the form

$$M^d = P + k_1 Y - k_2 \Delta P^e \tag{1}$$

where all variables are logarithms, M is the quantity of money, P an aggregate price index, Y denotes the level of economic activity and ΔP^e denotes the expected rate of inflation. Since we aggregate across countries, M is an index which weights together the individual money stocks of the various countries all measured in home currency units. A similar aggregation procedure applies to P and Y.

If the level of world economic activity is at its 'natural' level ($\bar{Y}$) equation (1) implies that the world price level will be proportionate to the world quantity of money. If there is an excess supply of money this will be associated with real balance effects which cause an excess demand for output so that $\dot{Y}$ exceeds $\bar{Y}$, or

$$Y = \bar{Y} + \alpha(M^s - M^d) \tag{2}$$

and the resultant demand pressures will trigger inflation. In addition, inflation will reflect the rate of increase of commodity prices which are imported by the 'world'. Hence

$$\Delta P = \beta_1(Y - \bar{Y}) + \beta_2 \Delta Z_1 + \beta_3 \Delta Z_2 + \beta_4 \Delta P^e \quad (3)$$

where Z_1 is the price of non-oil commodities and Z_2 is the price of oil. Z_2 is assumed to be exogenously determined by OPEC, and Z_1 is endogenous to the world economy.

If the quantity of money is fixed and the natural rate of output does not vary the expected rate of inflation in the steady-state will be zero, and commodity price shocks will only exert temporary effects on the price level and output. An increase in commodity prices will generate cost-push inflation via equation (3) which will depress demand via equation (2). However, the resulting recession will cause prices to fall until the recession has been eliminated. In the steady state the model implies

$$P = M - k_1Y + k_2 \Delta P^e$$

and $$\qquad\qquad\qquad\qquad\qquad\qquad\qquad\qquad (4)$$

$$Y = \bar{Y}$$

Aggregate Supply

So far we have assumed that the natural level of output is both fixed over time and unrelated to other variables in the model. The profit-maximising behaviour of competitive firms, see e.g. Bruno (1980), suggests that aggregate supply will vary inversely with real commodity prices since they are arguments in the cost function. If, in addition, the production function for Y is affected by disembodied technical progress, aggregate supply will be time-trended, assuming that technical progress can be proxied in this way.

Aggregate supply may be responsive to expected inflation but the effects are ambiguous. On the one hand it is arguable, e.g. Johnson (1976), that, as real capital replaces money balances in portfolios to hedge against inflation, aggregate supply will rise, since the capital stock is larger.

On the other hand, if real money balances are also arguments in the production function along the lines suggested by Friedman (1969) and Sinai and Stokes (1972), the lower equilibrium level of real balances will tend to depress aggregate supply. Therefore the sign of λ_3 in equation (5) cannot be determined on *a priori* grounds.

These considerations suggest that the natural level of output varies according to equation (5)

$$\bar{Y} = \lambda_1(Z_1 - P) - \lambda_2(Z_2 - P) + \lambda_3\Delta P^e + \lambda_4 t \qquad (5)$$

where t denotes an exponential time trend. This specification implies that an increase in real commodity prices will permanently contract the level of output and raise the price level via equation (4). Note that the natural rate of growth is not affected by such developments. Instead, the level of output is reduced on a once-and-for-all basis, although in practice this adjustment could be distributed over a number of years, during which time the rate of growth of output would be temporarily reduced.

Commodity Markets

The demand for non-oil commodities is assumed to depend on the level of economic activity and their relative price. If oil and non-oil commodities are gross substitutes in the production function, the demand for non-oil commodities will vary directly with the real price of oil as producers attempt to reduce their dependence on energy in favour of other commodity inputs. Therefore we may postulate equation (6) as the demand for non-oil commodities by producers

$$D = \gamma_1 Y - \gamma_2(Z_1 - P) + \gamma_3(Z_2 - P) + \gamma_4\Delta(Z_1^e - Z_1 - P^e + P) \qquad (6)$$

The last term represents the speculative demand for commodities. Since the real expected return on speculative inventories is $(Z_1^e - Z_1 - P^e + P)$, it follows that the flow demand for speculative inventories depends on the expected change in this real rate of return.

We postulate an upward-sloping non-oil commodity supply schedule. However, since energy is an input into the production process for non-oil commodities their supply will vary inversely with the real price of oil. Hence our supply hypothesis is

$$S = \gamma_5(Z_1 - P) - \gamma_6(Z_2 - P) + \gamma_7 t \qquad (7)$$

where the time trend reflects disembodied technical progress in the production function for non-oil commodities.

The equilibrium condition in the market for non-oil commodities is

$$D = S$$

which implies the following behaviour for real non-oil commodity prices:

$$\begin{aligned} Z_1 - P = (\gamma_1 Y + (\gamma_6 + \gamma_3)(Z_2 - P) \\ + \gamma_4 \Delta(Z_1^e - Z_1 - P^e + P) - \gamma_7 t)/(\gamma_2 + \gamma_5) \end{aligned} \qquad (8)$$

The price of oil Z_2 is exogenous and is assumed to be set by OPEC. Equation (8) implies that an increase in the price of oil raises commodity prices for two reasons. First, the cost of producing commodities rises. Secondly, the demand for commodities tends to rise.

Monetary Policy

To explain the rate of growth of the money supply we assume an aggregate government reaction function in which governments have an implicit trade-off between unemployment and inflation. As the world economy contracts, governments act to expand the rate of monetary growth with the intention of stimulating output. They are then hypothesised to reduce the rate of monetary growth as inflation increases in the hope that this will serve to reduce the rate of inflation.

These considerations suggest a reaction function of the form

$$\Delta M = -S_1(Y - \bar{Y}) - S_2 \Delta P \qquad (9)$$

To close the model we have to specify how expected inflation and expected non-oil commodity price movements are determined. Given the structure of the model the former might plausibly be related to the rate of monetary growth while the latter should reflect rates of change in Y and $Z_2 - P$ via equation (8).

For given assumptions about Z_2 the model solves for both short-run and long-run values for Y, P, M and Z_1. The long-run equilibrium of the model is described by equations (4), (5) and (8) for given assumptions about the money supply.

Econometric Estimates

Details of the econometric estimates may be found in Beenstock and Dicks (1981). An equation listing follows.

Output

$$\Delta Y_t = 1.952 - 0.54\,\Delta Y_{t-2} - 0.212\,\Delta Y_{t-3} - 0.412 Y_{t-4}$$
$$\quad (5.83)\quad (6.07)\qquad\quad (3.06)\qquad\quad (5.8)$$
$$\quad + 0.132\,\Delta_3 M_{t-3} - 0.212\,\Delta P_{t-2} - 0.705\,\Delta_2 P_{t-3}$$
$$\quad (1.93)\qquad\quad (2.22)\qquad\quad (11.33)$$
$$\quad + 0.33(M - P)_{t-6}$$
$$\quad (5.92)$$

$\bar{R}^2 = 0.8461$ $S = 0.0058$ $LM(5, 11.07) = 1.47$
$Q(4, 9.49) = 4.64$

Price level

$$\Delta P_t = 0.256 + 0.0021Q1 - 0.0018Q2 - 0.0011Q3$$
$$\quad (6.08)\quad (2.04)\qquad\quad (1.65)\qquad\quad (1.11)$$
$$\quad + 0.483\,\Delta P_{t-1} - 0.21\,\Delta_2 P_{t-2} + 0.069\,\Delta Z_{2t}$$
$$\quad (7.07)\qquad\quad (6.28)\qquad\quad (12.16)$$
$$\quad + 0.017\,\Delta Z_{1t} + 0.014 Z^*_{2t-1} - 0.126(P_{t-4} - M_{t-5})$$
$$\quad (1.59)\qquad\quad (4.7)\qquad\quad (6.34)$$
$$\quad - 0.0022t + 0.00058t$$
$$\quad (5.96)\qquad (3.46)$$

$\bar{R}^2 = 0.959$ $S = 0.0028$ $LM(5, 11.07) = 2.27$
$Q(4, 9.49) = 6.46$

Commodity prices:

$$\Delta Z^*_{1_t} = -6.29 + 0.1Q1 + 0.1Q2 - 0.1Q3 - 0.242\,\Delta_2 Z^*_{1_{t-1}}$$
$$\qquad (9.88)\quad (1.33)\quad (1.33)\quad (1.36)\quad (4.02)$$
$$\qquad - 0.46 Z^*_{1_{t-4}} + 1.545\,\Delta_3 Y_t + 0.54\,\Delta Y_{t-3} + 1.45 Y_{t-4}$$
$$\qquad\ (7.31)\qquad\quad (9.48)\qquad\quad (2.19)\qquad\quad (9.05)$$
$$\qquad + 0.109\,\Delta Z^*_{2_t} + 0.183 Z^*_{2_{t-3}} + 2.0\,\Delta^2 M_{t-1} - 0.022t$$
$$\qquad\ (4.5)\qquad\quad (8.73)\qquad\quad (3.17)\qquad\quad (8.55)$$
$$\qquad + 0.0052t'$$
$$\qquad\ (4.26)$$

$\bar{R}^2 = 0.768 \qquad S = 0.0195 \qquad LM(5, 11.07) = 8.09$
$Q(4, 9.49) = 2.42 \qquad Z^*_1 = Z_1 - P$

t^1 splits the exponential time trend t in 1969Q2

Money supply

$$\Delta M_t = 0.0127 + 0.338\,\Delta M_{t-1} + 0.167\,\Delta M_{t-2} - 0.072\,\Delta P_{t-1}$$
$$\qquad (5.23)\quad (2.99)\qquad\quad (1.6)\qquad\qquad (1.16)$$
$$\qquad - 0.134\,\Delta P_{t-2} - 0.112(Y - \bar{Y})_t + 0.00344 D$$
$$\qquad\ (1.76)\qquad\quad (5.72)\qquad\qquad (3.04)$$

$\bar{R}^2 = 0.7 \qquad S = 0.00345 \qquad LM(5, 11.07) = 2.92$

't' values are shown in parentheses. $LM(x,y)$ is the Lagrange multiplier test for randomness in the residual correlogram that has been proposed by Godfrey (1978), while $Q(x,y)$ tests for the constancy of the parameters of the model beyond the fitting period. Thus Q is essentially a test of outside sample performance. Both LM and Q have χ^2 distributions where x denotes the degrees of freedom and y the critical value of χ^2 at $p = 0.05$. The Q test refers to a post sample period of 1979Q1–Q4 with respect to the sample period of 1964Q1–1978Q4. If Q is satisfactory the model is then fitted over the whole period. D is a decreasing variable which is zero.

8

The Relative Economic Performance of the United Kingdom, 1950–80

Objectives

This chapter breaks with the precedent established in the rest of this book, by considering the economy of an individual industrialised country rather than the economies of the industrialised countries taken as a whole. The choice of the UK economy reflects the nationality of the author, but there is a less parochial reason too. During the 1970s the UK became a significant oil producer following the development of oil reserves in the North Sea. As luck would have it, the production of oil from the North Sea more or less coincided with the quadrupling of oil prices so that the real value of the oil output was increased and its effect on the UK economy was correspondingly different from what it might otherwise have been. Chapter 2 discussed the theoretical relationship between indigenous oil and raw materials production and the rest of the economy. Thus by considering the relative performance of the UK economy we may check whether any of these theoretical effects in fact materialised.

In addition the purpose of this chapter is to check whether the broad trends in the world economy that have been explained in terms of the Transition Theory have also been reflected in secular economic developments in the UK. If this is the case we may infer that secular trends in the UK economy may in part be understood in terms of the Transition Theory. As an integral part of the OECD bloc the UK is subjected to the same global economic forces that have affected the OECD bloc as a whole. However, there is no reason why the UK must be affected to the same degree as the OECD average or in precisely the same manner. It all depends on the structure of the UK economy, its relative factor intensities and the degree to which it trades with LDCs, and so on.

What we hope to achieve in this chapter is no more than a general overview of the economic performance of the UK relative to other countries over the period 1950–80. No detailed attempt is made to analyse the pattern of UK trade flows, factor intensities, etc. Indeed, the analysis is pitched at broadly the same level of aggregation as in the previous chapters of this book. The main findings are these:

- The secular trends in the UK economy by and large reflect those implied by the Transition Theory. However, the UK has been affected to a greater degree by these influences than the OECD bloc as a whole.
- In addition, North Sea oil production has driven a wedge between UK and OECD economic performance, especially with regard to the manufacturing and industrial sectors.

Output and the Real Economy

Figure 8.1 reveals that the deceleration in economic growth among OECD countries during the 1970s was also reflected in slower economic growth in the UK. The chart further reveals that economic growth is considerably more volatile in the UK than elsewhere although negative or less than

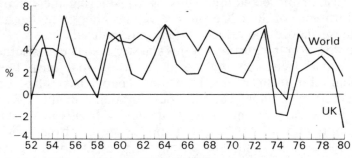

Source: National Accounts (Paris: OECD) various issues

Figure 8.1 *GNP growth rates 1952–80 in the UK and OECD ('world') (% p.a.)*

perfect positive correlation between individual country growth rates will reduce the variance of the OECD average. During the 1950s UK growth was 1.66 per cent per annum below the OECD average. During the 1960s it was 2.31 per cent per annum below the average and during the 1970s it was 1.95 per cent below. Therefore there is no indication that the deceleration in UK economic growth during the 1970s was out of line with the OECD average. In fact, the growth gap narrowed during the 1970s, relative to the 1960s, although part of this was due to the production of North Sea oil. By 1981 the share of oil production in GDP had risen to 5.85 per cent from zero in 1974.

Similarly Figure 8.2 reveals that the increase in UK unemployment during the 1970s broadly reflects labour market developments across the OECD as a whole. The data on Figure 8.2 have been standardised (by the OECD) and indicate that until the mid-1970s unemployment in the UK was typically lower than the OECD average. Since 1976 the converse has been true, and in 1981 it is estimated that the unemployment gap has jumped by several percentage points. In Chapter 4 it was noted that OECD unemployment began to rise during the second half of the 1960s, in accordance with the Transition Theory. A similar trend seems to

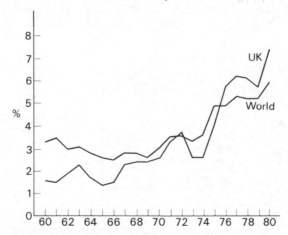

Sources: *National Accounts* (Paris: OECD) various issues
Labour Force Statistics (International Labour Office)

Figure 8.2 *Unemployment rates 1960–80 in the UK and OECD ('world') (% p.a.)*

apply in the UK. Previous research, e.g. by Maki and Spindler (1975), has sought to explain this phenomenon in terms of the effects of unemployment benefit on the 'natural' rate of unemployment. However, the present line of research indicates less parochial influences at work, although domestic phenomena might nevertheless have contributed to the growth of UK unemployment. Still, it is apparent from Figure 8.2 that the UK labour market has been more seriously affected by the world recession. This reflects either the greater exposure of the UK economy to structural change in the world economy, or the effects of the North Sea oil production as discussed below, or other domestic considerations.

Figure 8.3 enables us to compare net rates of return to fixed capital in manufacturing in the UK and OECD as a whole. Most probably, these differential rates of return reflect returns across capital as a whole rather than just the manufacturing sector. Although rates of return have drifted downwards in the UK, as elsewhere, there are some significant differences between the UK and OECD trends. First, the overall downward drift, both proportionately and absolutely, has been greater in the UK than elsewhere. Secondly, returns to manufacturing have been about ten percentage points lower in the UK, although much of this differential could be due to international differences in accounting conventions. Thirdly, the sudden downward break in returns

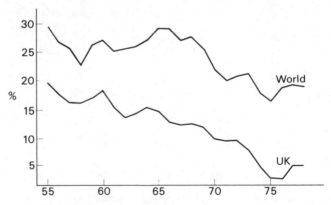

Source: Hill (1979), updated by OECD

Figure 8.3   *Net rate of return to fixed capital in manufacturing in the UK and industrialised countries ('world') 1955–78*

across the OECD as a whole during the late 1960s did not occur in the UK to the same degree. Nevertheless, it is evident that since the second half of the 1960s the downward trend in UK returns steepened. This suggests that Transition Theory effects were manifest in the UK and that the global factors that lowered returns across the OECD as a whole were exacerbating the downward trend in returns in the UK.

The causes of the underlying downward trend in returns to capital in the UK are imperfectly understood. One thesis is that restrictive practices of trade unions have resulted in the inefficient utilisation of capital which has lowered returns to capital. Another thesis, proposed by Sargent (1979), is that the postwar policy of capital subsidisation through investment allowances, etc., has lowered the net cost of capital to firms. The neoclassical investment model suggests that firms will tend to equate the marginal product of capital with its marginal cost. As the marginal costs of capital have been forced down by capital subsidies, additional investment takes place so that the returns to capital are forced down in line with the lower user costs of capital. According to this view, the secular decline in capital productivity in the UK is the result of capital subsidisation by government.

According to Figure 8.3, the OPEC oil price hikes of 1973–4 depressed capital returns in the OECD as a whole as well as in the UK. However, in both cases the returns to capital subsequently recovered, suggesting that higher energy prices resulted in only a temporary set-back to capital returns and profit shares (see Figure 8.4). This evidence seems to conflict with the findings of Berndt and Wood (1979), who argued that the production function is weakly separable in terms of capital and energy, as discussed in relation to Figure 2.6. In this case higher energy prices reduce energy demand by firms, with the result that the marginal product of labour is unchanged and the marginal product of capital declines. The fact that capital returns eventually stabilised by 1978 either suggests that the Berndt–Wood thesis is incorrect, or it implies that by 1978 the capital stock had fully adjusted to the new set of relative prices, i.e. the cost of capital and the returns to capital had been equated once more. Whatever the case, there is a striking parallel between the record of capital returns and profit shares in the

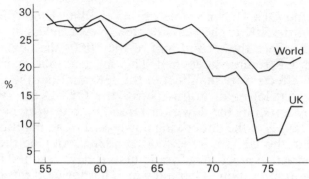

Source: Hill (1979), updated by OECD

Figure 8.4   *Profit share in manufacturing in the UK and industrialised countries ('world') (Net operating surplus ÷ net value added in manufacturing) 1955–78*

UK and the OECD as a whole over the period 1973–8. The data strongly suggest that structural economic developments in the UK must be understood in global rather than parochial terms.

There is, not surprisingly, a close affinity between the relative performance of the UK profit share and the relative performance of the rate of returns to capital in the UK manufacturing sector. Figure 8.4 indicates that, while the OECD profit share was stable during the 1950s and 1960s, it declined in the UK especially during the 1960s. It declined faster during the 1970s, but this reflected global developments which are to be understood in terms of the Transition Theory as already described.

A competing explanation of the faster decline in the UK profit share as from the late 1960s is that increased trade union pressure, supported by enlarged union membership rates, reduced profits to the advantage of wages. More aggressive trade union behaviour, it is hypothesised, inevitably forced down the profit share. As argued in Chapter 4, the Transition Theory can be used to explain the greater market power of labour as production as a whole becomes more labour intensive. The union-push hypothesis was, in any case, weak because it lacked a coherent theory of why the push began in 1969 rather than at any other time. Moreover, the findings of Layard, Nickell and Metcalf

(1978) suggest that trade unions had not succeeded (by 1973) in raising relative wage rates for their members. Therefore, in so far as a push hypothesis is valid it applies to the labour market as a whole rather than to trade unions in particular, and the greater market power of labour as a whole reflects Transition Theory effects.

De-Industrialisation and North Sea Oil

A major aspect of the Transition Thesis was that the manufacturing/industrial sector of the economy should have gone into relative decline during the late 1960s or early 1970s. In Chapters 3 and 4 de-industrialisation was measured by the share of industrial and manufacturing production in GDP. Figure 2.5 showed that this share had been rising across the developed world until the end of the 1960s, since when the share has faltered or even declined.

Figure 8.5 records the share of manufacturing and industrial output in UK output (excluding oil and gas production). The share rose steadily during the 1950s and 1960s and peaked in 1969. During the 1970s it fell very sharply, so that by 1980 it had returned to the level in 1948. Figure 8.5 also reveals that the decline in the second half of the 1970s was greater both absolutely and proportionately than the decline

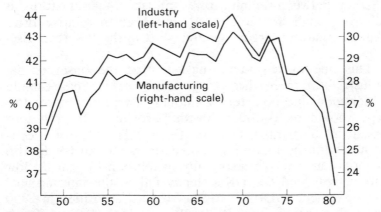

Source: Economic Trends (London: Central Statistical Office) various issues

Figure 8.5   *Industry's share of non-oil output in the UK 1948–81 (at 1975 prices)*

during the first half of the 1970s. In this respect the UK experience is at odds with that of the OECD as a whole. In relative terms the UK manufacturing sector has under-performed when compared with the OECD average during the second half of the 1970s.

It may be seen from Figure 8.5 that the proportionate rise in the manufacturing share over the period 1948–69 was greater than the proportionate rise in the share of industrial output. This experience mirrors the tendency across the OECD as a whole. Likewise, the proportionate decline in the manufacturing share during the 1970s was greater than the proportionate decline in the share of industrial output. This too mirrors OECD-wide experience. This is hardly sur-prising, because the Transition Theory essentially works through the manufacturing sector, for it is here that develop-ing countries have focused their industrialisation.

The fall in the manufacturing share in the UK in 1969 may be understood in terms of the Transition Theory, which has already been developed to account for the downward break across the OECD as a whole. However, it would seem that the downward break was much more pronounced in the UK than it was elsewhere. As argued above, there is no reason why the downward break in the UK should have been prop-ortionate to that in the OECD as a whole. The fact that it was greater suggests that the elasticity of substitution in pro-duction between manufactures and non-manufactures is relatively high in the UK, so that a given relative price change creates a larger resource shift in the UK than else-where.

This line of reasoning suggests that the onset of de-industrialisation in the. UK since the late 1960s can be understood in global terms. Global interpretations of this type should be contrasted with parochial interpretations based on the 'British Disease' theory. This theory is con-cerned with the relatively poor performance of the British economy as a whole, especially in relation to growth, low productivity and the UK's steady fall in the international league table of GDP per capita from third position in 1950 to twelfth position in 1980. Why growth rates differ is beyond the purview of the present exercise. Instead our con-cern is to explain *changes* in secular trends in the UK, and it has been argued that a global perspective is necessary to understand many changes that have recently taken place. However, the *level* of the trends may indeed be understood in more parochial terms and the 'disease' theory may be valid. I have no view either way on this thesis.

The disparity in the relative performance of the UK manufacturing sector since the mid-1970s requires a parochial interpretation. The main thesis to be proposed is that this additional degree of de-industrialisation is to be explained by the changing status of the UK as an oil producer. Table 8.1 records some basic facts about the UK's emerging role as an oil-producing country. Before 1975 oil production was zero. During 1980 the UK became self-sufficient in oil.

It was argued in Chapter 3 that if the UK is to benefit fully from North Sea oil the relative size of the traded goods sector must contract and the contribution of oil to the balance of payments must be offset by increased imports and reduced exports. The transmission mechanism runs as follows:

(1)   Increased oil production will tend to improve the current account.
(2)   If the exchange rate is floating, this will tend to raise the real exchange rate as the nominal exchange rate rises. If, instead, the exchange rate is fixed, UK wages and prices will tend to rise relative to prices abroad. In either case the real exchange rate rises.
(3)   As the real exchange rate rises, exports fall and imports rise.

Table 8.1   *North Sea oil and the UK economy*

	Oil production (millions of tonnes)	Share of oil production in GDP (% at current prices)	Net oil exports (£bn at 1975 prices)
1975	1	0.07	−3.35
1976	12	0.66	−3.25
1977	37	1.94	−2.09
1978	53	1.99	−1.64
1979	76	3.48	−0.81
1980	80	4.5	−0.05
1981	89	5.85	

(4) As exports fall, the size of the traded goods sector and thus the manufacturing sector contracts relative to the economy as a whole.

(5) The rise in the real exchange rate may be large or small, depending on the respective elasticities involved. The larger the increase, i.e. the smaller the elasticities, the greater the terms of trade benefit from North Sea oil. Therefore large increases in the real exchange rate are a blessing, rather than a curse. If resources are going to shift out of the traded goods sectors in any case, they may as well do so at higher rather than lower terms of trade gains.

Figure 8.6 plots the real exchange rate for sterling in terms of effective rates under various definitions. The chart shows, for example, that when the real exchange rate is defined in terms of relative wholesale prices the real value of sterling rose by about 21 per cent between the 1949 and 1967 devaluations, i.e. the 1967 devaluation did not restore the competitive position that prevailed after the 1949 devaluation. Between 1965 and 1975–6 there was a tendency for the real exchange rate to decline at an annual rate of approximately 1.9 per cent. This is precisely the trend rate of depreciation that has been incorporated into a number of econometric models of the UK economy, such as the Lon-

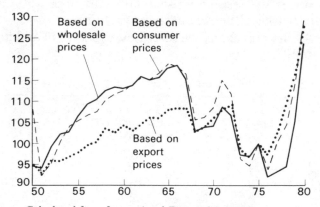

Source: Calculated from *International Financial Statistics*

Figure 8.6 *Measures of the real effective exchange rate for sterling 1950–80 (1975 = 100)*

don Business School's model. From Figure 8.6, however, it is clear that this trend is not suggested by examining a broader sweep of our economic history.

Since 1975 there has been a sharp upswing in the real exchange rate which broadly coincides with the profile of oil production from the North Sea (Table 8.1) and the profile of real oil prices (Figure 2.7). The suggestion is that the rise in the real exchange rate during the second half of the 1970s reflects the emergence of the UK as an oil-producing country. Forsyth and Kay (1980) estimate that the real exchange rate must appreciate by about 12 per cent by the year 1980 from what it otherwise would have been. On similar bases Beenstock, Budd and Warburton (1981) estimate a similar adjustment while Minford (1981) suggests that the real exchange rate effect of North Sea oil is likely to be much smaller.

As argued above, the scale of this adjustment only matters for calculating the terms of trade benefit from North Sea oil production. The main point is that oil trade must 'crowd out' non-oil trade in the balance of payments, whatever the real exchange rate effect happens to be. Evidence of this 'crowding out' process is suggested by Table 8.2. Table 8.2 shows that in real terms imports have grown rapidly during the period that Britain began to produce oil. In contrast exports grew sluggishly, at 1.7 per cent per annum between 1976 and 1980. The comparable rate of growth for non-oil imports was 4.8 per cent per annum. Another implication of Table 8.2 is that the improvement in the oil balance approximately mirrors the deterioration in the non-oil balance, as

Table 8.2 *'Crowding out' in the UK current account 1975–80 (£ millions at 1975 prices)*

	Non-oil exports	Non-oil imports	Net oil exports
1975	27174	25640	−3348
1976	29523	26839	−3251
1977	30985	27858	−2092
1978	31299	29217	−1644
1979	31729	33277	−808
1980	31640	32413	−55

Source: *Economic Trends* (London: Central Statistical Office) various issues

the 'crowding out' hypothesis suggests. Since Britain became an oil producer, by 1980 the oil balance had improved by about £3 billion at 1975 prices. Over the same period (1975–80) the non-oil balance deteriorated by £2.3 billion.

Figure 8.7 suggests that the growth in UK unemployment during the 1970s was largely concentrated in the manufacturing sector. Until 1980 the overall level of employment had been flat. However, by 1979 manufacturing employment had fallen by 14 per cent relative to its level in 1970, and by the second quarter of 1981 this decline had increased to about 27 per cent. By contrast, in the same quarter employment as a whole was only 5 per cent below its level in 1970. Therefore the shakeout of labour is essentially a manufacturing phenomenon.

Since 1977 there has been no growth in manufactured exports, i.e. the low growth in non-oil exports shown on Table 8.2 has been more pronounced in the case of manufactured exports. Normally, manufactured exports might be expected to grow in line with world manufactured trade. On this basis manufactured exports would have grown by 18 per cent between 1977 and 1980. This implies that in 1980 manufactured exports were 16 per cent below their normal level. Since manufactured exports are about 60 per cent of manufactured output we may deduce that the abnormally slow export growth resulted in a fall in manufactured output

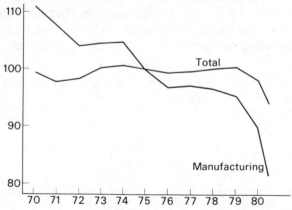

Source: *Employment Gazette* (London: DE) various issues
Figure 8.7   *Employment in the UK 1970–81 (1975 = 100)*

of approximately 10 per cent over the period 1977–80. Over the same period employment in the manufacturing sector fell by $7\frac{1}{2}$ per cent. These calculations suggest that the bulk of the decline in manufacturing employment can be explained by the hypothesis that North Sea oil adversely affects the manufacturing sector and that for a while mismatch unemployment increases.

This structural analysis of de-industrialisation in the UK since the mid-1970s should be contrasted with short-term analyses that blame the collapse of the manufacturing sector on monetary policies. These analyses turn on the relationship between monetary policy, the exchange rate and the manufacturing sector, and have been set out in great detail by the contributors to Eltis and Sinclair (1981). Most probably the truth is a mixture of the structuralist and short-term theories. My main objective has been to emphasise the structuralist interpretation which, hitherto, has gone largely unnoticed.

Long-Term Real Exchange Rate Movements

The previous discussion suggested that the rise in the real exchange rate, the slow growth of manufactured exports and the rapid import growth, and the decline in manufacturing output and employment during the second half of the 1970s were not a series of unrelated coincidences. On the contrary, these facts fit the basic theory about North Sea oil and de-industrialisation.

However, it is important to view the real exchange rate within a broader historical perspective. Figure 8.8 draws on Friedman's (1980) calculations of the real dollar–sterling exchange rate over the period 1868–1978. Note that, in contrast to Figure 8.6, a higher value implies a lower real exchange rate, following US conventions of measuring exchange rates as the reciprocal of the British practice. The chart reveals that between 1868 and 1939 the real exchange rate was not time-trended. However, there was considerable variation in the real exchange rate and deviations from PPP typically persisted for many years at a time. When Britain went off gold in 1932, the exchange rate rose in real terms (at least in relation to the dollar).

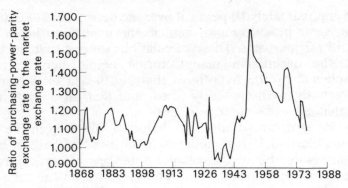

Source: Friedman (1980) Fig. 3.

Figure 8.8   *The Dollar–Sterling real exchange rate 1868–1978*

The behaviour of the real exchange rate since the second World War has been radically different to its previous history. The devaluation in 1949 pushed the real exchange rate to a historical low. The next fifteen years witnessed a recovery in the real exchange rate until the devaluation in 1967. The 1967 devaluation was not as severe as its 1949 precursor. Once again, however, this was followed by a recovery in the real exchange rate until sterling was floated in 1972. The real exchange rate fell but recovered after the mid-1970s. By the end of the period the real exchange rate had reverted to its long-run historical average.

This suggests that the rise in the real exchange rate since the mid-1970s is quite usual. It was simply an adjustment to its long run value. It also suggests that the UK monetary authorities have tried to keep an undervalued real exchange rate since 1949 and the market has responded by rejecting this policy. It is almost as if the high real exchange rate that materialised by 1980 was an equilibrium phenomenon rather than the disequilibrium phenomenon as it has come to be viewed.

On this basis the theory that the recovery in the real exchange rate in the second half of the 1970s was due to North Sea oil loses some credibility. This is an object lesson in the dangers of drawing inferences from relatively-short time series. The purpose here is not to reject the structuralist analysis but to pose a competing theory about the behaviour of the real exchange rate. The purpose is also to calm the nerves of real exchange rate alarmists who maintain that both the level and the rate of increase in the real exchange rate are unprecedented.

Inflation

The Transition Theory has no bearing on the rate of inflation. Nevertheless, this brief overview of the relative economic performance of the UK concludes by considering the UK's relative performance with respect to inflation. Figure 8.9 shows that since 1964 the rate of inflation in the UK has been higher than the average for industrialised countries. Until 1970 the discrepancy was small, of the order of one percentage point per annum. During the 1970s UK inflation has been completely out of line with inflation in the rest of the industrialised world. This has been made possible by the floating of the exchange rate in 1972. Although there is no reason why exchange rate flexibility should give rise to higher inflation, it is clear that the monetary authorities abused the greater degree of policy freedom afforded by flexible exchange rates to promote higher inflation.

The econometric model deployed in the previous chapter analysed inflation across the industrialised world in terms of money supply growth, commodity and oil price movements.

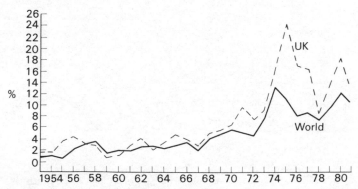

Source: *International Financial Statistics* (Washington, DC: IMF) various issues

Figure 8.9 *Consumer price inflation in the UK and industrialised countries ('world') 1953–81*

The latter are common to all industrialised countries, including the UK, although there is no reason why their effects should be the same in each industrialised country. In terms of the model, the main factor behind differential inflation rates are differential rates of monetary growth which can be independent across countries, especially when exchange rates are floating or devaluation is a realistic policy option. Figure 8.10 records the UK achievement with respect to differential monetary growth rates. It shows that during the 1950s and 1960s monetary growth was below the average for the industrialised countries. The upward drift in world monetary growth during the 1960s was reflected in an increase in monetary growth in the UK. By and large, until 1970 the profile of UK monetary growth was roughly in line with the profile of world monetary growth. This reflected the international transmission mechanism suggested by the monetary approach to the balance of payments which, under fixed exchange rates, implied that UK monetary growth had to fall into line with monetary growth abroad.

This theory does not imply that the level of UK and world monetary growth must be identical because of differential growth rates and trends in velocity. Figure 8.10 therefore suggests that the warranted rate of monetary growth in the UK is less than its counterpart in other industrialised countries, i.e. to maintain fixed exchange rates, monetary growth in the UK must be smaller than monetary growth abroad.

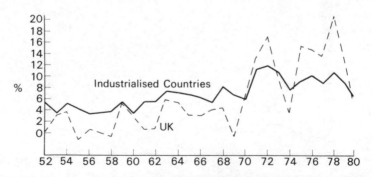

Source: International Financial Statistics (Washington, DC: IMF) various issues

Figure 8.10   *Monetary growth in the UK and industrialised countries 1952–80*

During the 1970s, and with the floating of sterling, the differential rate of monetary growth turned positive. Whereas before 1970 monetary growth was lower in the UK than elsewhere, the opposite has been true since 1970. The implication is that the differential rate of inflation during the 1970s is explicable in terms of the sharp increase in the differential rate of monetary growth.

The differential rate of monetary growth may in turn be explained in terms of differential rates of public sector borrowing. The thesis that monetary growth rates depend, in the medium term, on public sector borrowing has been promoted by Minford (1981) and Beenstock and Longbottom (1980). The basic insight is that if monetary growth were not proportionate to the growth in public sector debt, interest rates would either rise or fall without limit. They would rise without limit if the non-bank private sector was required to increase the proportion of public sector debt over time in its portfolio, which is what happens when monetary growth is less than the growth in public sector debt.

Unfortunately, it has not been possible to assemble data on differential rates of public sector borrowing. Instead, Figure 8.11 plots the government fiscal deficit as a proportion of GNP for the UK, on the one hand, and for an average of eight industrialised countries, on the other. Until 1964 the proportionate fiscal deficit in the UK was more or less in line with its overseas counterpart. Between 1964 and 1968 the

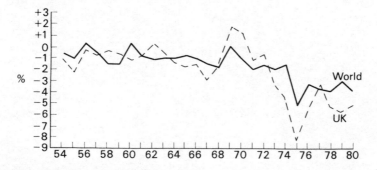

Source: *International Financial Statistics* (Washington DC: IMF) various issues

Figure 8.11 *Fiscal deficit as a proportion of GNP in the UK and 8-country industrialised 'world' 1954–80*
(deficit = −, surplus = +)

relative fiscal deficit rose but this was reversed over the period 1969–72. During the 1970s there were two important developments. First, the 'world' fiscal deficit rose by about two percentage points, especially in the wake of the 1973–4 oil price hikes. No doubt this was a major contributory factor to the higher monetary growth rates across the OECD as a whole during the 1970s. Secondly, the relative fiscal deficit in the UK increased (except for 1977). This suggests that the underlying explanation for the higher rate of monetary growth in the UK during the 1970s was the relative increase in the UK's proportionate fiscal deficit.

9

The Future of the International Economic Order

The New International Economic Order

This final chapter draws together the policy implications arising out of the previous discussion in this book. Since the Transition Theory is essentially concerned with the changing economic relationship between the rich and the poor countries, these policy issues are primarily concerned with the so-called New International Economic Order (NIEO). The debate about the NIEO is a child of the 1970s which to date has led to more frustration than fulfilment, and which has considerably soured international economic relations between rich and poor countries. Through the NIEO the poor countries have sought a realignment of economic power which the rich countries have refused to grant. Yet, curiously enough, it was the rich countries that allowed the debate to gather momentum in the first place, thus playing into the hands of the poorer countries who had sought this ever since the first UNCTAD conference in 1964.

The price policies of OPEC in 1973 caught the imagination of the 'non-aligned' nations who met in Algiers in September of that year. Could the LDCs form a united front to force concessions from the industrialised countries? A UN General Assembly was hastily convened in April 1974 and the Declaration and Program of Action of the New International Economic Order was adopted without a vote. This was the first time that the NIEO was formulated, although many of its demands were not new. In December 1974 the General Assembly formally threw down the gauntlet to the developed countries by approving the Charter of Economic Rights and Duties of States.

At this point the developed countries could have stonewalled the issue as they had done before at UNCTAD and similar gatherings. However, in the spring of 1975, Dr Kissinger, who was then US Secretary of State, essentially conceded the issue with the result that the seventh special session of the UN General Assembly was convened in September 1975. This session resulted in Resolution 3362, which endorsed many of the basic principles of the NIEO.

Ostensibly, Kissinger believed that if the oil crisis destabilised the Third World this might have incalculable political repercussions. Therefore it was in the interests of the capitalist rich countries to stabilise the economic and thus political orders of the day in the poorer countries. It is also conceivable that the initiative was designed to exert moral pressure on OPEC to lower oil prices, and thus to release the Third World from the economic hardships that had been thrust upon them. It also seems that Kissinger believed that the NIEO demands might be moderated, if the industrialised countries played along with the negotiations instead of distancing themselves. In view of what has happened subsequently there must be few initiatives that have backfired so sharply as the one launched by Kissinger in 1975; indeed, it is highly unlikely that the NIEO would have been born without his encouragement.

In December 1975 the Conference on International Economic Cooperation was formally established to consider fundamental reforms in international economic relationships between rich and poor countries in the areas of energy, trade, finance and commodity markets. LDC representatives pressed very hard for the establishment of various commodity price agreements, but the richer countries refused to co-operate. The Conference was eventually wound up in June 1977, having settled virtually nothing and having spread a cloud of acrimony between North and South.

This might have been the end of the matter. However, Mr McNamara, the then president of the World Bank, concerned that the failure of the Conference would leave a political vacuum, was instrumental in setting up the Independent Commission on International Development Issues under the chairmanship of Willy Brandt. The Brandt Commission, as it became to be known, published its findings in 1980 and called for a world political summit to see how various suggestions concerning the economic interdependence between North and South might be pursued. Despite a distinct lack of enthusiasm on the part of Mrs Thatcher and President Reagan, a summit was eventually held in Cancum (Mexico) in October 1981. Largely because of President Reagan's position, the summit failed to come to any substantial agreement and the politics of the NIEO have more or less run into the ground. At the time of writing (March 1982) an initiative by Mrs Gandhi to secure a united front amongst the South with which to confront the North has failed. So it appears that not even the developing countries can agree on what form the NIEO should take. The entire issue has become a veritable pandora's box, and predictably so. Is seems unlikely that the box will be closed for some considerable time.

Kissinger's concession to NIEO in 1975 was ill-conceived despite the best possible of intentions. On a personal note, at the time I happened to be attending some official meetings at the State Department in Washington DC, and it seemed clear that US officials were both surprised and disturbed by the announcement, certainly in the Treasury Department, but even within the State Department. Was this yet another instance of the 'Lone Ranger' style of diplomacy of which Kissinger was often accused?

Although there are some notable exceptions, such as Holland, the North by and large rapidly regretted the entire affair and hoped that it would quietly disappear. At the same time the South, under the leadership of the Algerians, did their best to ensure that this did not happen. Since it was fairly obvious that the debate about the NIEO was doomed to fail, it is surprising how much store political leaders of the South laid by it. Perhaps part of the explanation is that they found it a convenient scapegoat for their own economic problems which, all too often, had been brought about by unsuitable domestic policies rather than by the iniquities of the international economic order.

The Old International Economic Order

My main thesis is that the best international economic order is essentially the same as the one that prevailed in the early

1970s. And instead of fundamental reforms, what is needed is to preserve the old order which has been crumbling ever since. Despite progressive developments such as the Lomé Agreement, which gave signatory developing countries preferential trade treatment within the EEC, it is a curious irony that amidst all the clamour over the politics of the NIEO the benefits of the old order have been gradually eroded by the rise of the so-called 'new protectionism'. The old order, inspired by GATT and the IMF agreements, was founded on the principles of free trade and, to a lesser extent, free capital movements. If they wished to take advantage of it this afforded LDCs with the possibility of export-led industrialisation with respect to markets in industrialised countries. It also afforded them the opportunity of promoting such economic development on the back of capital that had been imported from the industrialised countries. Free trade and capital movements were the pillars of the old order and were vital to the spread of economic development. They are obviously not sufficient conditions for development, but they are almost sure to be necessary conditions.

Another feature of the old order was the transfer of resources to LDCs through economic aid. This has been a more controversial issue, since there are many who argue, e.g. Bauer (1976), that aid tends to strangle rather than to promote economic development. It sadly seems to be the case that, since aid is handled by LDC governments, it is often spent on prestige projects that at best do not further the economic development of the recipient countries and at worst hinder development. The latter occurs because aid covers capital costs only, and recurrent costs have to be borne by the government. Thus a prestige project tends to make deep inroads into the recurrent budget at the expense of support to more appropriate development projects. How depressingly familiar is the image of vehicles, machinery and equipment in the Third World that have been left to decay for want of elementary spare parts that the budget could not afford to finance.

UN targets to raise aid to 0.7 per cent of donor GNP have persistently failed although there are exceptions, e.g. Holland, which have unilaterally raised this target to 1 per cent. Table 9.1 reveals that the ratio of official development

Table 9.1 *The share of aid in OECD GNP 1960–80 (%)*

1960	0.51	1976	0.33
1965	0.49	1977	0.33
1970	0.34	1978	0.35
1975	0.36	1979	0.34
		1980	0.37

Source: World Bank (1981)

assistance (the OECD definition of aid) to GNP across the OECD as a whole has been roughly constant during the 1970s.

However, this represented a marked decline from the half per cent ratio that prevailed during the early 1960s. It was during the second half of the 1960s that aid performance sagged. Ironically, this coincided with the acceleration of growth in the LDCs. One possibility is that poorer donor performance reflects the growing scepticism about the contribution of aid to economic development. At least this can be deployed as an excuse for stinginess. Another possibility, based on the econometric analysis of aid flows by Beenstock (1980), is that donor governments find it politically necessary to reduce aid in line with reductions in public expenditure and when unemployment in donor countries rises. The explanation of the latter effect is that governments are pressurised to concentrate their charity at home rather than abroad. Thus the explanation for weakening aid flows lies in the gathering recession in the West and in more restrictive policies towards public expenditure. On this basis, aid in the 1980s is likely to remain unimpressive. But this is most probably a blessing in disguise, and it is a feature of the old order that is dispensable.

A slightly different picture emerges from Figure 9.1, which plots aid in real terms on a semi-logarithmic scale. The scale implies that the slope of the graph measures the rate of growth of real aid across OECD countries as a whole. The chart reveals that during the early 1960s aid grew relatively rapidly (the average growth rate over the period as a whole represented by the dotted line was $2\frac{1}{2}$ per cent per annum). However, from 1966 to 1974 aid was flat. During the second half of the 1970s real aid growth has been relatively rapid despite the stagnant performance implied by Table 9.1.

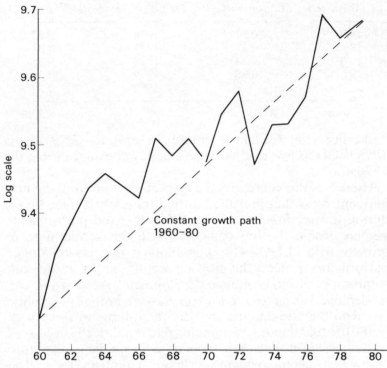

Source: *Development Cooperation* (Paris: OECD) various issues

Figure 9.1 *Official development assistance from OECD countries 1960–80 (at 1975 prices)*

The indispensable features of the international economic order are free trade and capital mobility. The main difference between the 'new protectionism' and the 'old' lies in the explicit nature of the latter and the surreptitious nature of the former. The rise of comprehensive protectionism in the 1930s was heralded as a fundamental economic panacea that was to be welcomed unashamedly and to be implemented across the board. In contrast, the growth of protectionism in the early 1970s and early 1980s has been more clandestine, *ad hoc* and discriminatory. Offending governments have evoked anti-dumping clauses in GATT to justify their actions, but it is clear that the spirit of GATT has been allowed to lapse. The Multi-fibre Arrangement, that sought to limit LDCs exports of synthetic and natural fibres and which was initially negotiated in 1972, was renegotiated, at the end of 1981. By this time it had become a coercive arrangement rather than a voluntary one, and it also extended its franchise to cover the textile trade as a whole. The object of this arrangement is to prevent LDCs from exploiting their newly-found comparative advantage in the production of textiles. Unlike the 'old protectionism', the 'new protectionism' is targeted at specific countries or groups of countries and at specific commodities or groups of commodities. It is therefore inevitably more discriminatory.

However, the 1970s also saw the resurgence of 'old protectionist' influences. In the UK, for example, there was pressure from the left wing of the Labour Party and from the Cambridge Economic Policy Group to apply comprehensive import controls. Both in the UK and elsewhere these factions were resisted, and although the world took a lurch towards protectionism this never materialised. One possible explanation for this lurch lies in the historically high degree of economic openness that has been achieved since the Second World War. Measuring economic openness by the ratio of exports plus imports to output at constant prices, Beenstock and Warburton (1981) show that openness rose gradually during the second half of the nineteenth century and reached a peak in 1930. Figure 9.2 illustrates this for the UK. Protectionist policies of the 1930s and the advent of the

Source: Beenstock and Warburton (1983)

Figure 9.2 *The ratio of trade to GDP in the UK 1870–1979 (at 1913 prices)*

Second World War destroyed the achievements of more than half a century in promoting economic openness. The establishment of GATT and the various tariff reduction 'rounds' in the postwar period has provided the basis for a restoration of economic openness. By the 1970s the degree of openness was more or less back at its peak level of forty years previously. This suggests that it is easier to destroy economic openness than it is to build up. This asymmetry reflects the fact that each country thinks that its protectionism will be unilateral and will not invite retaliation, whereas it is only prepared to remove its tariff barriers on a multilateral basis. In this way, protectionism spreads rapidly and is hard to reverse. This begs the following question: is it the case that political pressures for protectionism increase with the level of economic openness? It is almost as if the pressures in the 1970s reflect the pressures in the 1930s and that there is a maximum degree of openness which society can tolerate.

As for capital mobility the record has been much better. The tendency has been for capital markets to become more integrated internationally as exchange controls have been unwound and the euromarkets have developed. However, in many instances the attitude of some of the political leaders in the South regarding inward capital mobility has been ambivalent. On the one hand, they complain that they have unfair access to the world capital market and that capital inflows are inadequate. On the other, they resent private capital inflows, especially those associated with the investment of the multinationals. At one level, they recognise that the multinationals are propagating the spread of international development. If this were not the case the enormous growth in private inward direct investment could not have taken place. But at another level they resent the remittances of the multinationals as well as what the multinationals represent, namely the spread of capitalism. Thus far, however, the multinationals have not been frightened off, although there are instances where nationalisation and expropriation have achieved this. In so far as multinational activity in LDCs is to produce exports for industrialised country markets, attempts to limit DC–LDC trade are bound to reduce inward private direct investment.

Implications of the Transition Theory

A superficial interpretation of the Transition Theory might lead to the suggestion that is is in the interests of the developed countries to restrict imports from LDCs. Since the Transition Theory implies that slower economic growth in the West is related to manufactures-based industrialisation in LDCs, it might be deduced that the best thing the West can do is to frustrate this process in the first instance by trade restrictions which will adversely affect the prospects of the manufacturing sector in LDCs.

The conventional rebuttal of this protectionist thesis is that higher LDC GNP will generate a higher demand for DC exports. Therefore it is in the interests of the DCs to promote free trade and the development of LDCs. The implication here is that the jobs created by extra LDC imports from DCs will be greater than the jobs destroyed by LDC competition in international trade in manufacturers.

According to the Transition Theory, an increase in the level of economic activity in LDCs does not automatically bring about an increase in the level of economic activity in DCs, since aggregate supply is inelastic. The job creation effect takes for granted that labour supply is elastic. However, the most important implication of the Transition Theory is that in the medium term LDC economic growth can never result in unemployment in the DCs. At worst, there may be mismatch unemployment while the allocation of resources between different sectors of the economy adjusts. But it is in the nature of mismatch unemployment to be temporary rather than permanent. Once the resource allocation has adjusted to the new relative price pattern 'full employment' must prevail. Indeed, this hypothesis was corroborated at the end of Chapter 4.

A more appropriate interpretation of the Transition Theory would therefore reject the superficial case for protectionism mentioned above. In the medium term the level of employment would not benefit from protectionism. Instead, the main policy issue is how to minimise mismatch unemployment. Since mismatch is a reflection of rigidities in the labour and capital markets, this implies that policy should aim to reduce these rigidities. If labour and capital were perfectly mobile, mismatch could not exist. Resources would be reallocated across the economy without any frictions, and the economy would always be at its 'full employment' level irrespective of structural change. Most probably, frictions and rigidities are more pronounced in labour than in capital markets. To maximise the mobility of physical captial, second-hand markets must develop so that equipment can be moved from the declining manufacturing sector to the expanding sectors of the economy. This assumes that capital can be re-adapted for use elsewhere. For the most part, second-hand markets are most probably well developed and so there is no need for government involvement to expedite the mobility of physical capital.

By and large, the same applies to the mobility of financial capital, which is likely to be highly mobile between sectors. Expanding sectors of the economy find it easier to attract capital than contracting sectors. The crucial question is, do these differential capital movements fully reflect underlying economic considerations, i.e. is the capital market efficient? There is, of course, no comprehensive study of this issue; certainly not for the world as a whole. However, for the UK the Wilson Committee (1980) concluded that, except in the case of small businesses and housing finance the capital market was efficient. But one cannot generalise from this. The main point is that policy should be designed to remove whatever distortions are interfering with the basic efficiency of the capital market.

To some extent, policy has hindered this progress. In many instances governments have prolonged adjustment processes by supplying capital to declining sectors – the so-called 'lame ducks' policy. This has taken place through nationalisation, enterprise boards or direct subvention. Provided the capital market is efficient, these kinds of interventions are unnecessary, waste resources and increase resistance to economic change. Perhaps the first policy step is therefore to cease and reverse existing 'lame ducks' policies.

It is, or course, in the labour market that the most serious constraints to mismatch tend to arise. New jobs are not necessarily created in the same areas where the old jobs have disappeared. In the US the new jobs are being created in the southern states at the expense of the north-eastern states. In the UK jobs are disappearing in the Midlands but new jobs are being created in the Home Counties and East Anglia. Therefore the functional mobility of labour between jobs implies that labour must also be geographically mobile. It is one thing to switch jobs; it is quite another to switch addresses. Job switching may involve retraining. Industrial retraining has become a major issue. Should it be undertaken by the public or the private sector? What should be done in the case of middle-aged workers for whom retraining would be uneconomical? If the structure of wage differentials were flexible, the supply and demand for different types of labour would tend to balance out. The middle-aged unemployed could compete in the unskilled labour markets and this would be reflected in a fall in relative unskilled wage rates. If, however, wage differentials are made rigid by trade union restrictive practices, the employment prospects for such workers are reduced.

Mismatch unemployment adds to public expenditure, because those involved receive unemployment compensation. Therefore, in so far as retraining reduces mismatch there is an economic case to be made for subsidising such retraining. This, of course, is not the same as saying that retraining should be undertaken by the state.

Job switching may also involve substantial changes in work practices. There is growing evidence in the UK and the US that the new growth industries such as microelectronics are shunning unionised labour. It is partly for this reason that in the US these industries have been developing in the south, where trade unionisation is less entrenched. The degree to which these new industries can develop depends on the absence of restrictive practices, in which case mismatch is more likely to occur the greater the degree of unionisation, in terms both of enrollment rates and of restrictive practices.

Address switching may be constrained by inefficiencies in the housing market. In countries such as the US there are few barriers to mobility. In the UK the opposite is the case since, as noted by the Wilson Committee, the mortgage business is uncompetitive and the local authority housing system reduces the propensity to migrate, as noted by Hughes and McKormick (1981). To minimise mismatch the authorities must maximise mobility. Although this will vary from country to country, the principle issues most probably involve housing finance and public sector housing.

Other Implications of the Transition Theory

The Terms of Trade

Although the Transition Theory does not imply long-term unemployment in the developed countries, it does not suggest that economic welfare will not be adversely affected. The increase in the net aggregate supply of manufactures lowers the relative price of manufactures on world markets. Since DCs are net exporters of manufactures, their terms of trade deteriorate. This, indeed is the only longer-term disadvantage of LDC industrialisation.

Historically, policy makers have never based commercial policy on optimal tariff arguments which hinge upon the exploitation of terms of trade movements. It is therefore unlikely that politicians would pay any attention to calls for trade restrictions against LDC manufactured exports on these technical grounds. Instead, the evidence suggests that they would be prepared to take such restrictive action when jobs are threatened and it is largely for this reason that the Multi-fibre Arrangement was renegotiated. The sole preoccupation was with jobs rather than the terms of trade. However, it has already been argued that this was (and still is) inappropriate.

Third World Indebtedness

The Brandt Report considers the scale of LDC indebtedness as a potential threat to world economic stability. If enough LDCs defaulted, banks would default and the world monetary system might crash. We may draw some comfort, therefore, from the Transition Theory in so far as it suggests that the growth of LDC indebtedness is an equilibrium phenomenon which reflects their stage of development. This does not imply that individual Third World countries are not causes for concern. Rather it suggests that there is no aggregative debt problem and that there is no fundamental threat to world monetary stability. A default need not result in an epidemic.

There is, however, the danger that talk of instability will be self-fulfilling. In this case a default will result in an epidemic not because of any economic justifications but because of unjustified fears of bankruptcy. There is nothing to fear but fear itself. Perhaps if it is realised that the growth of LDC indebtedness is a natural consequence of their quest for development some of these fears will be seen in a broader perspective.

The Future Prospect

Economists are notorious for their explanations of the past and infamous for their forecasts of the future. After the event we may tell our different stories, some perhaps more inspired than others, but before the event we tend to be relatively speechless. This book has essentially been a story of the past; it has been an attempt to piece together an entire range of economic developments within a comprehensive theoretical framework. However, it is extremely doubtful that the author could have predicted all these developments in advance. Therefore the Transition Theory is essentially an *ex post* invention which readers may or may not find convincing.

No scholar is ever totally persuaded by his theories. In presenting new theories he tends to overstate his case somewhat out of fear that the fledgling will not otherwise get the chance to fly. This is certainly true of the spirit in which the Transition Theory has been presented in this book. What has impressed me is not the individual elements of evidence on profit shares, rates of returns to capital, de-industrialisation, relative prices, capital movements, unemployment, growth, etc. Instead it is the totality of evidence from two centuries that is impressive – that all of these variables have moved as the Transition Theory implies. It is the more or less clean sweep of the theory that catches the intellectual eye, rather than the explanations of individual developments which often are not very spectacular. It is this that recommends the theory for serious consideration.

The main exogenous variable in the Transition Theory is LDC industrialisation. Had the author been forewarned in the early 1960s that a few years later LDC industrialisation would take place, *ex ante* predictions could have been made along the usual *ceteris paribus* lines. In terms of the Transition Theory the economic prospects of the industrialised countries depend on whether and at what pace industrialisation will spread to the relatively backward LDCs. Should we regard the success of the so-called newly industrialised countries as a once and for all event, or should we regard it as an event that will keep repeating itself until all the world has industrialised? In the former case there is only a once and for all adjustment to be made on the part of the industrialised countries. In the latter case adjustments will continue as long as industrialisation keeps spreading.

Most probably, the domino theory of economic development is more appropriate and more and more countries in the Third World will, for good or evil, step onto the treadmill of economic growth and development. It is only a matter of time before even backward countries like Mali join Korea and Brazil in the quest for development. However, it is unlikely that the spread of development will be uniformly distributed over time. Just as in the late 1960s there emerged a first generation of NICs, it is possible that new NICs will come in future generations too. Whatever the time distribution of economic development, it is surely daunting to think that thus far we have seen no more than the tip of a great iceberg. On the whole, the first generations of NICs were small countries and involved no more than 300 million people from the Third World. This leaves 1860 million to be touched by the development process, or 2860 million if we include China. This is the equivalent of 520 Hong Kongs!

After a century, the balance of world economic power in the 1960s began to shift in favour of the developing countries. The greatest challenge to the world economic order is coming to terms with the inexorable spread of economic development over the next hundred years. It will be as much a test of the integrity of man as it is a challenge to policy makers.

Bibliography

Abramovitz, M. (1964) 'The passing of the Kuznets cycle', *Economica*
Aldcroft, D. H. (ed.) (1968) *The Development of British Industry and Foreign Competition, 1875–1914* (London: Allen and Unwin).
Bacon, R. and Eltis, W. A. (1980) *Britain's Economic Problem: Too Few Producers* 2nd Edition, (Macmillan).
Baily, M. N. (1981) 'Productivity and the services of capital and labour', *Brookings Papers on Economic Activity*, vol. 1.
Balassa, B. and associates (1971) *The Structure of Protection in Developing Countries* (Baltimore, Md: Johns Hopkins University Press).
Balassa, B. (1981) *The Newly Industrialising Countries in the World Economy* (Oxford: Pergamon).
Bank of England (1982) 'North Sea oil and gas: a challenge for the future', *Bank of England Quarterly Bulletin*, March.
Barron, I. and Curnow, R. (1979) *The Future with Micro-electronics* (London: Francis Pinter).
Batchelor, R. A., Major, R. L. and Morgan, A. D. (1980) *Industrialisation and the Basis for Trade* (Cambridge: Cambridge University Press).
Bauer, P. T. (1976). *Dissent on Development* (London: Weidenfeld and Nicolson).
Beenstock, M. (1977) 'Policies towards international direct investment: a neoclassical reappraisal', *Economic Journal*, September.
Beenstock, M. (1979) 'Do U.K. labour markets work?', *Economic Outlook*, June/July.
Beenstock, M. (1980) *A Neoclassical Analysis of Macroeconomic Policy* (Cambridge: Cambridge University Press).
Beenstock, M. (1980) 'Political econometry of official development assistance', *World Development*, January.
Beenstock, M., Budd, A. and Warburton, P. (1981) 'Monetary policy, expectations and real exchange rate dynamics', *Oxford Economic Papers* (Suppl.) July.
Beenstock, M. and Dicks, G. (1981) 'An aggregate dynamic monetary model of world output and prices', forthcoming in *European Economic Review*.
Beenstock, M. and Longbottom, A. (1980) 'The statistical relationship between public sector borrowing and the money supply in the United Kingdom', *Economic Outlook*, July.
Beenstock, M. and Minford, A. P. L. (1976) 'A quarterly econometric model of world trade and prices' in M. Parkin and G. Zis (eds.), *Inflation in Open Economies* (Manchester: Manchester University Press).
Beenstock, M. and Warburton, P. (1982) 'An aggregate model of the UK labour market', *Oxford Economic Papers*, July.
Beenstock, M. and Warburton, P. (1983) 'Long-term trends in economic openness in the United Kingdom and the United States', *Oxford Economic Papers*, March.
Beenstock, M. and Willcocks, P. (1981) 'Energy consumption and

economic activity in industrialised countries: the dynamic aggregate time-series relationship', *Energy Economics*, October, pp. 225–37.

Berndt, E. and Wood, D. (1979) 'Engineering and econometric interpretations of energy-capital and complementarity', *American Economic Review,* June.

Bhagwati, J. (1958) 'Immiserising growth: a geometric note', *Review of Economic Studies,* June.

Billerbeck, K. and Yasugi, Y. (1979) 'Private direct foreign investment in developing countries', *World Bank Staff Working Paper,* no. 348, July.

Brandt, W. *et al.* (1980) *North–South: A programme for Survival* ('The Brandt Report') (London: Pan Books).

Bruno, M. (1980) 'Import prices and stagflation in industrialised countries', *Economic Journal,* September.

Bruno, M. (1981) 'Raw materials, profits and productivity slowdown', *National Bureau of Economic Research Working Paper 660,* April.

Bruno, M. and Sachs, J. (1979) 'Macroeconomic adjustment with import price shocks: real and monetary aspects', *National Bureau of Economic Research Working Paper 340.*

Bruno, M. and Sachs, J. (1981) 'Supply versus demand approaches to the problem of stagflation', *Weltwirtschaftliches Archiv.*

Byatt, I., Hartley, N., Lomax, R., Powell, S. and Spencer, P. (1982) 'North sea oil and structural adjustment', *Government Economic Service Working Paper* No. 54, (London: H.M. Treasury) March.

Cable, V. (1978) 'Source of employment displacement in UK industries competing with LDC imports', mimeo (London: Overseas Development Institute) April.

Cairncross, A. K. (1953) *Home and foreign investment 1870–1913* (Cambridge: Cambridge University Press).

Chenery, H. and Syrquin, M. (1975) *Patterns of Development 1950–1970,* Oxford University Press

Cole, H. S. D. (ed.) (1973) *Thinking About the Future* (London: Chatto and Windus).

Coppock, D. J. (1956) 'The climacteric of the 1890s: a critical note', *The Manchester School,* pp. 1–31.

Cornwall, J. (1977) *Modern Capitalism: its Growth and Transformation,* (Oxford: Martin Robertson).

Davidson, J. E. H. *et al.* (1978) 'Econometric modelling of the aggregate time series relationship between consumers' expenditure and income in the United Kingdom', *Economic Journal,* December.

Deane, P. and Cole, W. A. (1969) *British Economic Growth 1688–1959,* 2nd ed. (Cambridge: Cambridge University Press).

Delbeke, J. (1981) 'Recent long wave theories: a critical survey', *Futures,* August.

Eden, R. *et al* (1981) *Energy Economics: Growth, Resources and Policies* (Cambridge: Cambridge University Press).

Eltis, W. A. and Sinclair, P. J. N. (eds) (1981) *The Money Supply and the Exchange Rate,* (Oxford: Clarendon Press).

Feinstein C. H. (1972) *National Income, Expenditure and Output of the United Kingdom 1855–1965,* Cambridge University Press.

Flanders, M. J. (1964) 'Prebisch on Protectionism: an Evaluation' *Economic Journal*, June.

Foreign and Commonwealth Office (1979) 'The Newly Industrialising Countries and the Adjustment Problems', *Government Economic Service Working Paper*, No. 18 (London: FCO).

Forsyth, P. and Kay, J. (1980) 'Economic Implications of North Sea oil revenues', *Fiscal Studies*, July.

Freeman, C. (ed.) (1981) *Futures* August and October.

Friedman, M. (1980) *Prices of Money and Goods across Frontiers: the Pound and the Dollar over a Century* (London: Trade Policy Research Centre).

Fröbel, F., Heinricks, J. and Kreye, O. (1980) *The New International Division of Labour*, (Cambridge: Cambridge University Press).

Gerschenkson, A. (1962) *Economic Backwardness in Historical Perspective*, (New York: Praeger).

Godfrey, L. (1978) 'Testing for higher order serial correlation in Regression Equations when the Regressors include lagged dependent Variables', *Econometrica*, November.

Havrylyshn, O. and Wolf, M. (1982) 'Promoting trade among developing countries: an assessment', *Finance and Development*, March.

Helleiner, G. K. (1979) 'Structural aspects of Third World trade: some trends and prospects', *Journal of Development Studies*, April.

Heal, G. M. and Dasgupta, P. S. (1979) *Economic Theory and Exhaustible Resources*, Cambridge Economic Handbooks, Nisbett.

Hicks, N. (1976) 'A model of trade and growth for developing countries', *European Economic Review*, pp. 239–55.

Hill, T. P. (1979) *Profit and Rates of Return*, OECD, Paris.

Hughes, G. and McCormick, B. (1981) 'Do council housing policies reduce migration between regions?', *Economic Journal*, December.

Imlah, A. H. (1958) *Economic Elements in the Pax Britannica* (Cambridge, Mass.: Harvard University Press).

International Monetary Fund (1981) *External Indebtedness of Developing Countries*, Occasional Paper 3 (Washington DC: IMF) March.

Jevons, W. S. (1866) *The Coal Question*, 2nd ed. (London: Macmillan).

Jewkes, J., Sawyers, D. and Stillerman, R. (1969) *The Sources of Invention*, 2nd ed. (London: Macmillan).

Johnson, H. G. (1976) 'Money in a neoclassical one sector growth model', *Essays in Monetary Economics* (London: Allen and Unwin).

Kahn, H. (1979) *World Economic Development* (London: Croom Helm).

Kemp, M. C. (1969) *The Pure Theory of International Trade and Investment* (Engelwood Cliffs, NJ: Prentice-Hall).

Kendall, M. G. and Stuart, A. (1968) *The Advanced Theory of Statistics*, Vol. III, (London: Charles Griffin).

Kondratieff, N. V. (1935) 'The long waves in economic life', *Review of Economics Statistics*, November.

Kreuger, A. O. (1980) 'LDC manufacturing production and implications for OECD comparative advantage' in I. Leveson and J. W. Wheeler (eds.) *Western Economies in Transition* (London: Croom Helm).

Kuznets, S. (1961) *Capital in the American Economy* (Princeton, NJ: Princeton University Press).

Kuznets, S. (1966) *Modern Economic Growth,* (New Haven, Conn: Yale University Press).

Labys, W. C. and Granger, C. W. J. (1970) *Speculation, Hedging and Commodity Price Forecasts* (Lexington: D. C. Heath).

Layard, P. R. G., Nickell, S. and Metcalf, D. (1978) 'The effect of collective bargaining on relative and absolute wage rates', *British Journal of Industrial Relations,* pp. 287–302, November.

Leamer, E. E. (1978) *Specification Searches* (Chichester: Wiley).

Lewis, W. A. (1949) *Economic Survey 1919–1939* (London: Allen and Unwin).

Lewis, W. A. (1978a) *The Evolution of the International Economic Order,* (Princeton, NJ: Princeton University Press).

Lewis, W. A. (1978b) *Growth and Fluctuations 1870–1913* (London: Allen and Unwin).

Lewis, W. A. (1980) 'The slowing down of the engine of growth', *American Economic Review,* September.

Lucas, R. (1972) 'An equilibrium model of the business cycle', *Journal of Political Economy.*

MacDougall, G. D. M. (1960) 'The Benefits and Costs of private investment abroad: a Theoretical Approach', *Economic Record.* Vol. 36, pp. 13–35.

Madison, A. (1977) 'Phases of capitalist development', *Banca Nazionale del Lavoro Quarterly Review,* June.

Maki, D. and Spindler, Z. A. (1975) 'The effects of unemployment compensation on the rate of unemployment in Great Britain', *Oxford Economic Papers,* October.

Malinvaud, E. (1977) *The Theory of Unemployment Reconsidered* (Oxford: Blackwell).

Meadows, D. H., Meadows, D. L., Randers, J. and Behrens, W. W., III (1972) *The Limits to Growth* (New York: Universal).

Mensch, G. (1979) *Stalemate in Technology* (Cambridge, Mass: Ballinger).

Minford, A. P. L. (1980) 'Government borrowing fans inflation', *Journal of Economic Affairs,* October.

Minford, A. P. L. (1981) 'The exchange rate and monetary policy', *Oxford Economic Papers* (suppl.).

Morawetz, D. (1971) *Twenty-Five Years of Economic Development* (Baltimore, Md: Johns Hopkins University Press).

OECD, *The Impact of the Newly Industrialising Countries on Production and Trade in Manufactures* (Paris: OECD).

Panic, M. and Enoch, C. A (1981) 'Commodity prices in the 1970s', *Bank of England Quarterly Bulletin,* March.

Phelps Brown, E. H. and Handfield Jones S. J. (1952) 'The climacteric of the 1890s: a study in the expanding economy', *Oxford Economic Papers,* October.

Phelps Brown, E. H. and Hopkins, S. V. (1956) 'Seven centuries of the prices of consumables compared with builders' wage rates', *Economica,* November.

Prebisch, R. (1964) *Towards a New Trade Policy for Development* (New York: UN).

Rostow, W. W. (1960) *The Stages of Economic Growth* (Cambridge: Cambridge University Press).

Rostow, W. W (1978) *The World Economy* (London: Macmillan).

Rostow, W. W. (1979) *Getting from Here to There* (London: Macmillan).

Rostow, W. W. (1980) *Why the Poor get Richer and the Rich Slow Down* (London: Macmillan).

Rybczynski, T. M. (1955) 'Factor endowment and relative commodity prices', *Economica,* November.

Sabot, R. H. (1978) *Economic Development and Urban Migration* (Oxford: Clarendon Press).

Sachs, J. D. (1981) 'The current account and macroeconomic adjustment in the 1970s', *Brookings Papers on Economic Activity,* Pt. 1.

Sargent, J. R. (1979) 'Productivity and profits in UK manufacturing', *Midland Bank Review,* Autumn.

Saul, S. B. (1969) *The Myth of the Great Depression, 1873–1896,* (London: Macmillan).

Schmookler, J. (1966) *Invention and Economic Growth* (Cambridge, Mass: Harvard University Press).

Schumpeter, J. A. (1934) *The Theory of Economic Development* (Cambridge, Mass: Harvard University Press).

Shirk, G. (1975) 'Another item in the 54-year Cycle Study', *Cycles* Vol. 26, No. 3 Foundation for the Study of Cycles Incorporated Pittsburgh Pa.

Simon, M. (1968) 'The pattern of new British portfolio investment 1865–1914' in A. R. Hall (ed.) *The Export of Capital from Britain* (London: Methuen).

Sinai, A. and Stokes, H. (1972) 'Real money balances, an omitted variable from the production function', *Review of Economics and Statistics,* pp. 290–6.

Spraos, J. (1980) 'The statistical debate on the net barter terms of trade between primary commodities and manufactures', *Economic Journal,* March.

Stolper, W. F. and Samuelson, P. A. (1941) 'Protection and real wages', *Review of Economic Studies,* pp. 58–74.

Stout, D. K. (1979) 'De-industrialisation and industrial policy' in F. Blackaby (ed.) *De-industrialisation* (London: Heinemann).

United Nations Center on Transnational Corporations (1980) *Transnational Corporation Linkages in Developing Countries* (New York: UN).

United Nations Industrial Development Organisation (UNIDO) (1981) *World Industry in 1980* (New York: UN).

van Duijn, J. J. (1977) 'The long wave in economic life', *De Economist,* pp. 544–76.

Vernon, R. (1966) 'International investment and international trade in the product cycle', *Quarterly Journal of Economics,* pp. 190–207.

World Bank (1981) *World Development Report 1981* (New York: Oxford University Press).

Index